## Praise for Barrie Barton

"Barrie's expertise in streamlining content, organizing my ideas and aligning the slides was remarkably efficient and on point. Her coaching gave me the benefit of feeling confident in my content and relaxed in my delivery."
—RICHARD FORT, ARCHITECT

"Barrie helped me turn my speech from boring to brilliant! She has a wonderful way of capturing my essence and plugging it into my flat, science-based speech. Barrie taught me how to shine brightly when presenting my research. I am truly grateful for all that I learned from her."
—AIMEE WILLIAMS, BUSINESS OWNER

"My conference speech was a massive hit. Over 1,300 people heard it, and probably 200 people came up to me and told me how much they enjoyed it. I couldn't have done it without Barrie!"
—BRENT DARNELL, EMOTIONAL INTELLIGENCE COACH

"Barrie Barton was instrumental in helping me deliver a very successful TEDx talk. She's an inspiring and thoughtful coach. If you do any public speaking in your life I highly recommend working with her."
—KAT HOUGHTON, ECO-THERAPY COACH

"I tend to get overwhelmed/immersed in details/research and have trouble with outlining it and boiling it down. Barrie really helped get me arrow-focused on the points of my talk."
—Nancy Casey, Scientific Programmer, Riverside Technology, Inc., at NOAA's National Centers for Environmental Information

"Barrie Barton is an ahh-mazing speaker coach. She just coached me through the process of doing my first TEDx talk and I truly do not know what I would have done without her. If you want to take your speaking skills to the next level . . . no matter where you are, her program will do it. And it'll be fun!"
—Jen Aly, money coach for creatives

"Working with Barrie was simple and straightforward and had a powerful effect on me: on my comfort level, my belief that I can bring our message to the world. I appreciated her low-stress delivery style, the simple strategies for preparing that she taught us, and her generosity of spirit."
—Cheri Torres, CEO of Collaborative by Design

"I want to tell everyone just how helpful the coaching session with Barrie was. I went in unsure what to expect and came out with helpful and actionable ideas to incorporate into my talk. Barrie is amazing!"
—Astra Coyle, Feldenkrais practitioner

# ABOUT THE AUTHOR

**Barrie Barton** is dedicated to the art and strategy of personal and professional communication and presentation. She founded the speaking coaching and facilitation company Stand and Deliver in Asheville, NC, in 2015, and has helped hundreds of businesspeople, architects and engineers, artists, and thought leaders learn to communicate their ideas with clarity and passion.

Barrie also teaches public speaking at UNC Asheville, and, through Next AVL, mentors local college students in pitch design and delivery. In 2019 she served as coaching coordinator for TEDx Asheville and is now the event's Executive Director.

Barrie holds a BA in Dance from the University of California, Santa Barbara, and a Master of Arts Education from Vermont College. She brings this extensive artistic training to her role as artistic director of Story Choreography Projects. Established in 2006, Story Choreography Projects invites participants to artful play, explore, and express and express themselves through movement, stories, creative writing, and choreography.

*"My greatest joy is helping others discover their innate ability to express themselves, guiding them in enhancing and refining their skills and talents, and providing a platform for them to shine.*

*"My goal is to empower, guide and inspire my clients to reach their fullest potential. Whether you want to craft and deliver a speech, pitch to potential clients, or perform your authentic stories, this book should help you find your voice, craft a meaningful and memorable message, and share your gifts with the world."*

**TWICE 5 MILES GUIDES**
**the stuff nobody teaches you**

*Also in this series*

HOW TO EDIT AND BE EDITED:
and polish your work to a professional shine
by Allegra Huston

HOW TO READ FOR AN AUDIENCE:
and touch people's hearts
by James Navé and Allegra Huston

How to
# MAKE A SPEECH
and inspire your audience

Barrie Barton

**Twice 5 Miles**

Taos • London

copyright © 2022

All rights reserved. No part of this book may be reproduced in any form or by any electronic or mechanical means, including information storage and retrieval systems, without permission in writing from the publisher except by a reviewer, who may quote brief passages in a review. Scanning, uploading, and electronic distribution of this book or the facilitation of such without the permission of the publisher is prohibited. Please purchase only authorized electronic editions, and do not participate in or encourage electronic piracy of copyrighted materials. Your support of the author's rights is appreciated. Any member of educational institutions wishing to photocopy part or all of the work for classroom use, or anthology, should send inquiries to Twice 5 Miles, P.O. Box 2999, Taos NM 87571, or info@twice5miles.com.

ISBN 978-0-9857528-8-0 (paperback)
ISBN 978-0-9857528-9-7 (e-book)


Twice 5 Miles
P.O. Box 2999
Taos, NM 87571

twice5miles.com

Book design by Kelly Pasholk, Wink Visual Arts
Cover design by Alex Alford, Colourfield

# CONTENTS

**Let's Get Started** . . . . . . . . . . . . . . . . . . . . . . . . . . . . . . . 1
    The Desire to Inspire . . . . . . . . . . . . . . . . . . . . . . . . . . 1
    Overcoming the Fear. . . . . . . . . . . . . . . . . . . . . . . . . . . 3
    How to Use This Book . . . . . . . . . . . . . . . . . . . . . . . . . 5

**Chapter 1: Discover Your Message**. . . . . . . . . . . . . . . . . 7
    The Lake of Your Ideas. . . . . . . . . . . . . . . . . . . . . . . . . . 8
    The Seven Key Questions . . . . . . . . . . . . . . . . . . . . . . . 10
        Key Question 1: "What's my motivation?". . . . . . . . 11
        Key Question 2: "Who are my listeners?" . . . . . . . . 13
        Key Question 3: "What do I want my listeners
        to do, feel, or believe?" . . . . . . . . . . . . . . . . . . . . . . 18
        Key Question 4: "What's the one thing
        I want my listeners to remember?" . . . . . . . . . . . . . 21
        Key Question 5: "What do my listeners
        need to know?" . . . . . . . . . . . . . . . . . . . . . . . . . . . 25
        Key Question 6: "Why me?". . . . . . . . . . . . . . . . . . 26
        Key Question 7: "How much time do I have?". . . . . 27

**Chapter 2: Compose Your Speech** . . . . . . . . . . . . . . . . . 32
    Gather Your Treasures. . . . . . . . . . . . . . . . . . . . . . . . . 32
    Start Writing Your Speech . . . . . . . . . . . . . . . . . . . . . 34
        Splat it. . . . . . . . . . . . . . . . . . . . . . . . . . . . . . . . . . 34
        Speak it. . . . . . . . . . . . . . . . . . . . . . . . . . . . . . . . . 35
        Map it. . . . . . . . . . . . . . . . . . . . . . . . . . . . . . . . . . 37

**Chapter 3: Shape Your Speech** . . . . . . . . . . . . . . . . . . 38
   The Speechwriter's Hourglass. . . . . . . . . . . . . . . . . . . 39
   The Basic Building Blocks of a Speech. . . . . . . . . . . . . 41
      Opening . . . . . . . . . . . . . . . . . . . . . . . . . . . . . . . . 41
      Why me?. . . . . . . . . . . . . . . . . . . . . . . . . . . . . . . . 49
      Core message . . . . . . . . . . . . . . . . . . . . . . . . . . . . 49
      Why does it matter? . . . . . . . . . . . . . . . . . . . . . . . 54
      Key points. . . . . . . . . . . . . . . . . . . . . . . . . . . . . . . 56
      What's possible? . . . . . . . . . . . . . . . . . . . . . . . . . . 60
      Call to action . . . . . . . . . . . . . . . . . . . . . . . . . . . . 62
      Closing . . . . . . . . . . . . . . . . . . . . . . . . . . . . . . . . . 70

**Chapter 4: Animate Your Speech** . . . . . . . . . . . . . . . . . 75
   Quotes. . . . . . . . . . . . . . . . . . . . . . . . . . . . . . . . . . . . 76
   Story . . . . . . . . . . . . . . . . . . . . . . . . . . . . . . . . . . . . . 77
   Data. . . . . . . . . . . . . . . . . . . . . . . . . . . . . . . . . . . . . . 79
   Transitions. . . . . . . . . . . . . . . . . . . . . . . . . . . . . . . . . 82
   Audience Participation . . . . . . . . . . . . . . . . . . . . . . . 84
   Q & A . . . . . . . . . . . . . . . . . . . . . . . . . . . . . . . . . . . . 87
   Slides . . . . . . . . . . . . . . . . . . . . . . . . . . . . . . . . . . . . . 92

**Chapter 5: Polish Your Speech** . . . . . . . . . . . . . . . . . . 97
   How to Time Your Speech . . . . . . . . . . . . . . . . . . . . . 97
      Techniques for cutting . . . . . . . . . . . . . . . . . . . . . 98
   Adding Flavor. . . . . . . . . . . . . . . . . . . . . . . . . . . . . . . 99
      Metaphor . . . . . . . . . . . . . . . . . . . . . . . . . . . . . . . 99
      Humor . . . . . . . . . . . . . . . . . . . . . . . . . . . . . . . . 101
      Repetition. . . . . . . . . . . . . . . . . . . . . . . . . . . . . . 103
   Assess Your Progress. . . . . . . . . . . . . . . . . . . . . . . . . 106
      The value of pauses . . . . . . . . . . . . . . . . . . . . . . 109

## Chapter 6: Rehearse Your Speech . . . . . . . . . . . . . . . 111
Create a Customized Speech Map . . . . . . . . . . . . . . . 111
Memorization . . . . . . . . . . . . . . . . . . . . . . . . . . . . . . . . 114
    Using notes . . . . . . . . . . . . . . . . . . . . . . . . . . . . . . 115
Polish Your Delivery . . . . . . . . . . . . . . . . . . . . . . . . . . 119
    Establish a pre-performance routine. . . . . . . . . . . 119
    Practice your speech . . . . . . . . . . . . . . . . . . . . . . 121
    Rehearsal techniques . . . . . . . . . . . . . . . . . . . . . . 125

## Chapter 7: Deliver Your Speech . . . . . . . . . . . . . . . . . 129
Preliminary Checklists . . . . . . . . . . . . . . . . . . . . . . . 129
    Prepare Your Introduction . . . . . . . . . . . . . . . . . . 132
    What to Wear. . . . . . . . . . . . . . . . . . . . . . . . . . . . 133
    Speak Like a Pro. . . . . . . . . . . . . . . . . . . . . . . . . . 135

## Chapter 8: Speaking on a Virtual Platform . . . . . . . . 137
Let Us See You . . . . . . . . . . . . . . . . . . . . . . . . . . . . . . 137
    Background. . . . . . . . . . . . . . . . . . . . . . . . . . . . . . 138
    Lighting . . . . . . . . . . . . . . . . . . . . . . . . . . . . . . . . 139
    Camera position . . . . . . . . . . . . . . . . . . . . . . . . . 139
    What to wear . . . . . . . . . . . . . . . . . . . . . . . . . . . . 141
Let Us Hear You . . . . . . . . . . . . . . . . . . . . . . . . . . . . . 141
    Tech . . . . . . . . . . . . . . . . . . . . . . . . . . . . . . . . . . . 142
    Tone . . . . . . . . . . . . . . . . . . . . . . . . . . . . . . . . . . . 142
Additional Tips. . . . . . . . . . . . . . . . . . . . . . . . . . . . . . 143

## Chapter 9: Honoring Someone You Love . . . . . . . . . 144
Gather Your Treasures. . . . . . . . . . . . . . . . . . . . . . . . 145
Craft Your Toast . . . . . . . . . . . . . . . . . . . . . . . . . . . . 146
    Choose the right story to tell . . . . . . . . . . . . . . . . 147

Shape Your Toast. . . . . . . . . . . . . . . . . . . . . . . . . . . . 148
Polish Your Toast. . . . . . . . . . . . . . . . . . . . . . . . . . . . 150
Prepare to Perform . . . . . . . . . . . . . . . . . . . . . . . . . 150
    Practice the toast. . . . . . . . . . . . . . . . . . . . . . . . . . 151
Deliver Your Toast. . . . . . . . . . . . . . . . . . . . . . . . . . . 152
What to Avoid. . . . . . . . . . . . . . . . . . . . . . . . . . . . . . 154
Words of Love. . . . . . . . . . . . . . . . . . . . . . . . . . . . . . 156

**Appendix: Sample Speech Shapes** . . . . . . . . . . . . . . 157
The Basic Hourglass . . . . . . . . . . . . . . . . . . . . . . . . . 157
Compare and Contrast . . . . . . . . . . . . . . . . . . . . . . . 159
Chronological . . . . . . . . . . . . . . . . . . . . . . . . . . . . . . 162
Speech to Honor Someone . . . . . . . . . . . . . . . . . . . . 165

# Let's Get Started

## The Desire to Inspire

Are you a businessperson, preparing to present your product or service to an outside audience?

Are you a team leader, ready to inspire your colleagues to address a new challenge?

Are you a researcher, a campaigner, or a nonprofit executive, excited by the opportunity to share your ideas at a conference, a fundraiser, or an event such as TEDx?

Are you an artist or writer, presenting your work at a gallery opening, book launch, film festival, or play premiere?

Maybe you'll be accepting an award of some kind. You could just say "thank you" and sit down again—but that would be missing an opportunity. You have a platform, for a couple of minutes, to convey the importance of the work that earned you this award, and to win converts or collectors or clients.

Or maybe there's a family occasion coming up: a wedding, bar mitzvah, or memorial service. You are there to celebrate someone you love. You want to express that love to listeners who may not know the person (or people) as well as you do. You want to describe what delights you about them, what makes them special in your eyes. You want others to feel your gratitude for their presence in your life, now or in the past. Perhaps you want to express your hopes for their future. Above all, you want create a swell of warmth and appreciation that will carry your loved one, or loved ones, into the next phase.

Whether your goal is to motivate action, to drive sales, to spur creativity, to explain the value of your work, or to build good feeling and community, all effective speeches have one thing in common: the desire to inspire. Your speech has the power to influence opinion, emotion, policy, and action—if you craft it well and deliver it with authenticity and passion.

The desire to influence and inspire your listeners is the engine of your speech. It gives your speech purpose. Without a desire to make an impact on your audience, your speech will be flat and forgettable. So, the first thing you must do, right now, is to ask yourself this question:

*What action, emotion, desire, or opinion
do I want to inspire in my listeners?*

Heartfelt words are a powerful tool, in private settings as well as public. When I was a child, my father said to me, "I believe people are basically good." This little speech stuck, and ever since it has influenced how I see the world and interact with others. Throughout history, leaders in all walks of life have used words to better society, to drive change, to help people weather catastrophes. Of course, great speakers have used words for evil ends, too. But in accordance with my father's words, I will assume that your intentions are good.

I have two goals in this book: to give you the tools to inspire and influence your listeners, and to motivate you to put your passion or hope or belief into words and take it out into the public arena. Now is the time to embrace your inner confidence and seize the opportunity to inspire action, influence decision-makers, communicate ideas, celebrate accomplishments, or let potential customers know about your valuable product or service.

Though I will use presentation-type speeches as my primary examples, the techniques I present in this book apply equally to speeches made at weddings or other family occasions. These speeches, too, aim to inspire and to communicate an idea to an audience, and they have a clear opening, body, and closing. And, most definitely, they benefit from rehearsal and a confident delivery.

## Overcoming the Fear

Jessica came to me for speech coaching. She was in the process of publicizing a book she'd written, which had a brilliant idea at its center. She had reams of notes for her speech; she'd done all her homework. But even though she'd only booked one session, she seemed not to want to work on her speech. "I just want to brainstorm today," she told me. After 15 minutes, I said, "Jessica, I'm just curious. Are you wanting to brainstorm today because you have a fear of really getting the speech together?" As soon as I said the word "fear," Jessica started to cry. She admitted that she was afraid of putting her ideas out into the world.

We were never going to end up with a powerful speech if Jessica was afraid of sharing her ideas with passion and confidence. So the first step was to gather a small group who were willing to listen to Jessica offer her ideas—a mini audience, so that Jessica could break through the fear.

The fear of public speaking is well known, and maybe you suffer from it. Many people do—and many people overcome it because they want to celebrate a loved one or convey their passion in art or business or social policy. I find that the fear of public speaking is not just a question of performance anxiety. Many people are also afraid of how the content of their speech will be received.

Sharing ideas you're passionate about makes you feel vulnerable. You worry: Is this going to be relevant? Is this going to be interesting? Have a zillion people already said this, better than I can say it? The fear of not being taken seriously stops people in their tracks.

Pulling together a mini audience before even starting to craft your speech, as Jessica did, is a great first step. Then, once you start crafting it, stay in the creative process. Don't let your mind jump ahead to the picture of you standing on a stage facing an audience expecting a dynamo speech that you're not sure you can produce. As you make your way through this book and come to understand how a good speech is put together, you may worry that your skills aren't up to working with such a smart system. Maybe it's too demanding; maybe you can't do it well. You can! It's a step-by-step process. You might not hit it out of the park on your first try—but on the other hand, you might! Making a speech, like pretty much everything, is something you get better at with practice.

---

*Tip: Stay in the moment as you craft your speech*

---

There are people who can just wing it. They craft a speech pretty much by instinct. One woman came to me for coaching, saying, "I've given lots of speeches but I realize I don't really know what I'm doing." It was hit or miss for her—more hits than misses, for sure, but even so, she wanted to bring greater conscious awareness to the craftsmanship of speechmaking. Not having a clear grasp of what she was doing was preventing her from reaching the next level.

Another important factor in building your confidence is doing your due diligence—making sure you are completely in command of your subject and your material. Just as you wouldn't sell a house without putting in the windows and doors, you don't want to stand in front of an audience without having made sure your speech is as solid and watertight as that well-built house. This will go a long way toward settling your nerves.

In chapters 6 and 7, when we talk about rehearsing and delivering your speech, I will give you further techniques to put yourself in a mental place of calm and confidence. Even a tiny modicum of comfort will get you through!

## How To Use This Book

There is no single "correct" formula for crafting an excellent speech. You might be toasting your best friend at their wedding, discussing your art practice at a Pecha Kucha, sharing your expertise in a business setting, or promoting a cause at an event such as TEDx. Each of these speeches has a different purpose, so each requires a different style.

Every audience is different, and so is every speaker. We all have an innate ability to express ourselves, but the ways in which we process information, apply our expressive style, and share our gifts with others are individual to each one of us. After years of teaching adults, college students, and even elementary school students, I've come to respect that individuality. So, when I coach people on how to make a speech, I encourage them to follow their own distinct approach to generating ideas, organizing content, and connecting with their listeners.

Having said that, all good speeches share a basic architecture, and all take account of seven key questions. First, we'll investigate those questions, since it's important to consider them before you begin to compose your speech. We'll follow that with approaches to finding your message, ways to organize your speech from start to finish, how to polish and rehearse it, and, finally, how to deliver it.

As you'll discover, designing a speech is both a strategic and a creative endeavor. I trust you to know when to take the creative road and when to turn onto the strategic path. As you read this book, follow your own personal approach. You may prefer to learn how to craft a speech page by page, step by step. Or you may benefit from a more digressive approach, reading in whatever order best builds your understanding. I invite you to explore and experiment.

Tap into your creativity. Try using brightly colored markers and sticky notes. Make a collage of images. Draw pictures. Discover your own personal way to make this creative expression fun.

My clients take wildly differing paths as they create and craft their speeches. Not all the techniques in this book will work for you—but every technique will work for someone.

You have something to share with the world, your community, your colleagues, and your friends. Step strongly into your brilliance. Think big. Offer your gifts.

*Creativity is intelligence having fun.*
—Albert Einstein

# 1

# Discover Your Message

Okay, so there's a speech in your future. How do you start? Do you sit down to write it, mug of coffee beside you and fingers hovering over the keyboard?

Please don't. That is actually one of the last steps in the process of crafting a speech with the power to influence and inspire your listeners.

A well-crafted speech is the product of experimentation: some trial and plenty of error. We start with raw material: an intention, ideas for stories or lines of argument that might be included, maybe some rough data. Much of your material may not connect up. Maybe you feel that you don't have enough material but aren't sure where to find more. You might already know what you want your listeners to do, or have a plan of action you want to impart—or that may remain to be discovered. Very possibly you don't know where to start, or finish, or both.

That's fine. You're not supposed to know any of this when you begin. You know you're making a speech, and you know your topic. That's enough for now.

In the process of crafting your speech, you'll investigate your audience, you'll hone in on your purpose, and you'll come to a clear understanding of what you most want to say. As you work with your material, you'll discover the main thread of your ideas, and that will guide you in deciding which stories or lines of argument will make the greatest impact, and how best to connect your stories, arguments, and motivation with the stories, experiences, and motivations of your listeners.

## The Lake of Your Ideas

Imagine that your ideas are a lake. You swim in this lake with ease, because you know its currents and its depths. You understand how your ideas flow. You know where your ideas stand on a solid foundation—where the lake bottom is visible—and where there are depths you haven't fully explored.

When you give a speech, you invite your listeners to swim in this lake.

Most people's tendency, especially when time is short, is to plunge their listeners straight in. You want to immerse them in your thoughts, your beliefs, your goals, but it's easy to forget that they may not be able to swim in the lake of your ideas the way you can.

When an audience comes to hear you speak, they are on the shore of that lake. Some may already be dipping their toes into the water, since they know your topic and want to hear what you have to say. Others who are less engaged (because they're distracted by personal worries, waiting for the next speaker, or any number of other reasons) need to be coaxed even to pay attention.

Calling to them from the center of the lake—where your ideas are most exciting to you—certainly won't work for these people. It doesn't even work for the people who are already interested. Yet this is what most speakers do. They begin speaking from within their ideas, rather than meeting their listeners on the shore—that is, at the place where your ideas and your listeners' experience meets—and inviting them in.

Kamala works for Dogwood Alliance, an environmental nonprofit, and was preparing a speech on how environmental justice issues affect the lives of low-income communities in North Carolina. When she delivered her first draft at my Speaker's Learning Lab, I was thrown immediately into stormy waters. Waves of conservationist jargon crashed over my head. Data flew by like sea-spray. There was no sight of land—no sense of where we were going—because there was no clear call to action. Nor did I understand why she wanted me to join her on this wild ride.

When you throw your listeners into a tempest, their first reaction is to seek safety. They pull back. They see no reason why they should join you. They stop listening.

Obviously, this is not what Kamala intended. She was not hearing what her audience was hearing.

As you read this book, you will learn how to meet your listeners where they are, excite their interest, and guide them into the lake of your ideas. You cannot acquaint them with every molecule of water in the lake, but you can chart a course and give them an idea of the lake's geography. You can point out the most appealing features of the far shore—the end result you are hoping to achieve—and you can suggest possibilities for further discovery. An effective speech leaves your listeners with the desire to come back to this lake in the future—perhaps by reading your book, visiting your website, watching a video, or taking some other action that you propose.

## The Seven Key Questions

Grab a notebook and pen. You are going to answer seven key questions. These seven questions serve like a sculptor's chisel, helping you carve away the excess and discover, clarify, hone and polish the message you want to impart.

Jot down your answers, and any ideas they bring up, as you go along. This is the first step in developing a speech.

The first four questions will help you develop your **core message**. This is not the same thing as the topic of your speech. Your core message—or, as TED calls it, your big idea—focuses your topic in such a way as to inspire and influence your listeners. It combines your expertise, experience, and insight with a message the audience needs, or wants, to hear. This message is threaded through your entire speech, beginning to end.

Perhaps there's a problem to which you have a new solution. Perhaps you can offer a fresh understanding of a subject on which you are an expert. Perhaps you're introducing a plan or strategy to your team, and you want them to understand its value. Perhaps you want to affirm that this marrying couple are perfect for each other.

> *"You need a tangible idea to get you going. The idea, however minuscule, is what turns the verb into a noun – paint into a painting, sculpt into sculpture, write into writing, dance into a dance."*
>
> —Twyla Tharp

And also, what turns speaking into a speech.

## Key Question 1: "What is my motivation?"

Everyone who makes a speech has a reason for making it. In business, you might be offering a service, selling a product, motivating a team, or bidding for a contract. Or you might be promoting your work or your passion, advancing a cause, or celebrating a loved one.

What is your own personal, specific motivation for making this speech, at this time? Why are you putting yourself in front of an audience? And why this audience, in particular?

Let's get super clear on *your* personal "why."

We are all motivated by personal benefit. For the most part, everything we do is done because we expect some sort of positive outcome for ourselves. You wouldn't be planning to make this speech (however unwilling and nervous you might feel right now!) if you didn't believe that in some way it will create positive value. For you.

> *"Achievement happens when we pursue and attain what we want. Success comes when we are in clear pursuit of why we want it."*
> —Simon Sinek, inspirational speaker and author of *Start with Why*

So, let's imagine your ideal outcome. If you give the best speech you possibly can, will you:

- convert listeners to clients
- enlist partners in an undertaking
- engage people in a cause
- put your topic on the political agenda

- get publicity for your work
- expand understanding of your work
- get your proposal accepted
- fund your project
- share your artistic vision
- foster a group feeling of love and appreciation

Feel that intent, strongly and clearly. Write it down so you can read it. Say it out loud. Sit with it until you know it in your bones.

Now, change the channel.

Our creative spirit is embedded in personal motivation. But if your personal motivation leads your speech, you will sound like a salesperson. You may convince a few of your listeners, but you'll alienate the majority of them.

*Having* a personal motivation is very different from *leading* with it. Most people can sense very quickly when a speaker is leading with self-motivation, and they don't like it. Why? Because their motivation is the same as your motivation: to derive a positive outcome for themselves. They aren't there for your benefit; they're there for their own.

You cannot simply transfer your own motivation to your listeners. Motivation has to arise naturally. Most people are motivated by passion, so your task is to ignite a spark of your passion in your listeners. By clarifying your motivation, proudly claiming it, and then placing the focus on your listener's outcome, you will gain the bandwidth to inspire them.

Return to what you wrote in your notebook, and add a second part to your motivation. Ask yourself, "What do I want for my listeners?" Express this outcome for your listeners by inserting "so they will ___."

Be specific; give your listeners a motivation they can connect to.

For example, you might want to:

- engage your listeners in a cause, *so they will* change the unfair policies affecting our children
- convert your listeners to clients, *so they will* become more empowered in their professional endeavors
- fund your project, *so they will* trust that the water they drink is clean
- share your artistic vision, *so they will* see the world with new eyes
- accept your proposal, *so they will* receive the best product available and first-rate customer service

Your motivation turned outward empowers your speech to be a conduit of your expertise offered for the benefit of your audience. As speakers, we are leaders. Good leadership is servant leadership, so our role is to serve our listeners. That generosity of spirit is the mark of a great inspirational speaker.

### Key Question 2: "Who are my listeners?"

Speaking is an act of connection. You are reaching out from your depth of expertise, experience, and conviction in order to influence or inspire others with a message that they will find personally relevant and perhaps useful in their path in life or work.

You might think it's manipulative to guess what's going on inside someone else's head and craft your speech accordingly. I assure you it's not. Good communication—whether formal or informal, and whatever its motivation—always stays sensitive to the listener.

You are giving this speech because you believe that in some way your material has value for your listeners. You want them to see that value. So you must understand, as fully as possible, why they would care about your topic. What will compel them to pay attention?

Recently, I was asked to give a speech to the monthly meeting of an organization that serves human resources professionals. No topic was specifically requested, so I led with my expertise: how to give a speech.

In my years as a speaker's coach, I have taught hundreds of people to give speeches, so this was an easy speech for me to write. I detailed the steps in writing a speech and the techniques for delivering one. I rehearsed my speech in front of a group of friends, who praised it as well crafted and well delivered. But in my gut, I knew something was wrong.

Because it was so easy for me to do, I had written a speech about what I knew—not about what my listeners wanted to hear. I had not met my listeners on the shore of the lake of my ideas and invited them in. What I had done was toss them into the deep part, with no floaties.

This is a common trap. We all love our expertise. I could talk about effective speaking, and different approaches to designing a speech, for hours. But I'll never reach my listeners if I don't take account of their perspectives, their interests, their needs. Instead of asking, "What do I know about this subject?" (in other words, what's in it for me), I need to ask, "Why should my listeners want to know about this subject?" In other words, what's in it for them.

---
## Tip: Enter your audience's world
---

The next day, I got on the phone and interviewed friends who work in human resources. I asked them to detail the tasks of their day. I asked them to tell me their satisfactions and their struggles.

Guess what? Most human resources professionals don't spend their days giving speeches. In fact, speechmaking is pretty far down the list of what they believe they'd find helpful in their job. And speechmaking was my topic. So, my challenge was to figure out why my audience should give a damn.

This is what I realized: even though they're not making speeches, human resources professionals spend a large amount of their time talking. Much of their workday is taken up by communication with employees and executives, and much of that communication is verbal, face-to-face. Understanding this gave me the makings of a speech that would be relevant, and useful, to my listeners.

I titled my speech "Take a Seat at the Leadership Table," in order to convey to my listeners, before I even started speaking, that they would learn something from my speech which would benefit them in their professional lives. Early on, I said, "Giving speeches isn't your day-to-day world." By acknowledging that my topic might seem irrelevant to my listeners, I met them where they were—on the shore of the lake. Then I explained why my topic was, in fact, very relevant to them. Drawing from my phone interviews, I listed some of the circumstances in which a human resources professional would be called upon to speak clearly and concisely, with facts and figures, imparting motivation and inspiration—and, often, without much warning.

- "You're unexpectedly called into an executive's office to explain the vacancy rate."
- "You're talking with a staff member about policy implementation."
- "You're reviewing programs with a group of managers."
- "You're training your team."
- "You're recruiting new talent and interviewing for open positions."

By saying, "You're," I was directly addressing my listeners. By listing these various situations, I was saying to them, "I understand your world. I understand what you do in the course of a day, and what your needs are."

Then, I refocused the body of my speech away from "how to give a speech" toward the larger topic of verbal communication. Using stories, good and bad examples, and descriptions of techniques, I illustrated how strong communication skills could enhance my listeners' professional effectiveness, influence, and opportunity.

In other words, I made clear what was in it for them.

### How Do You Learn About Your Audience?

First of all, **don't** assume you know all there is to know about the people who will be listening to you speak—even if they're your team members engaged in a project you all understand.

And, if you'll be speaking to a general audience, such as at a TEDx presentation or community event, **don't** assume there is nothing specific to know.

Here are some questions to ask:

- Will these people be there because they have a specific interest?
- Do they want to be there, or is it compulsory?
- What is their general level of education?
- Is this a regionally defined audience, who will connect to certain regional topics or experiences?
- How is my topic relevant to these people's lives?

If an organization has hired you to make this speech:

- What is its business?
- What is its history?
- Does it have a stated mission and vision?
- What connection do its representatives see between you and their organization?
- Is there a particularly pressing problem they are experiencing as an organization, or as a segment of the general population? Are there solutions or avenues of exploration that you can suggest?

Taking the time to consider and research these questions will ensure you are speaking to your audience's agenda rather than to your own.

Answer these questions by:

- calling colleagues or acquaintances who have first-hand experience with your future audience, or might in theory be members of it
- researching the organization on the internet
- interviewing current or former executives, employees, and/or clients (it's good manners to ask the person who hired you to arrange these conversations)
- interviewing actual members of your future audience (on occasion I have sent, with permission from the organization, a simple survey to clarify for myself what my audience will be expecting)
- If you are able to see who is attending through pre-registration, find out a little more about these people who have signed up to hear you. What are their interests? Work and education experience? Age range?
- If you are speaking at a family celebration, learn more about the families—and make sure you know the name of everyone you'll be referring to!

When you demonstrate early in your speech that you understand your listeners' experience and concerns, they will be more willing to believe that your words have value for them.

## Key Question 3: "What do I want my listeners to do, feel, or believe?"

Your listeners will take their seats, or stop chatting, with an expectation: to be motivated, informed, compelled, opened up, amused, educated. They are anticipating an experience that will be memorable in some way. Perhaps they will see their life, or their friends and family, in a new light. Perhaps they will be given a vision, or receive direction, from a leader. Perhaps a new venture may seem possible. Perhaps their perceptions of some aspect of their everyday world will be changed.

Do you want your listeners to:

- be inspired so they will take action on a political, environmental, or personal subject?
- understand a new perspective on something?
- agree to hire your company?
- implement new business strategies?
- change their behavior or adopt a new behavior?
- gain new knowledge?
- discover a method to make their business more successful?
- feel motivated to take the next step for business, financial, or self-improvement?
- share your respect, delight and/or appreciation for a person, a place, or an activity?

Here's an example. An architect asked my advice on a speech he would be delivering to his colleagues about an upcoming design competition. His content, which described the technical challenge of the competition and the procedure for entry, was well organized, and his delivery was powerful and clear. But the speech lacked motivational fire.

"What do you want your listeners to do?" I asked him.

"I want the junior members of our firm to enter the competition," he replied.

He had told them what the competition was. He had told them how to enter it. But he was not telling them why they might want to spend their time and imagination on this challenging competition. His speech was focused on the wrong priority. He was not meeting his listeners on the shore of the lake.

In fact, there were two excellent reasons to enter the competition: a monetary prize, and substantial prestige for the winner and the firm as a whole. He had included this information—right at the end. So, as it stood, his speech was unlikely to engage his listeners until after the information they needed had passed them by. The fix was simple: move the information that would engage and motivate his listeners to the beginning of the speech, and then tell them how to achieve the goal.

The answer to "What do I want my listeners to do?" is the basis for your **call to action**. The call to action is the response to your core message. We will discuss the call to action in more detail later.

Knowing what you want your listeners to do helps you zero in on the message you want them to take away from your speech. Thus, the core message of my architect client's speech changed from "there is an important design competition coming up" to "you will benefit from entering this important design competition coming up."

Here are some more examples:

- If you are changing a major system in your organization:
  - Do you want your listeners to feel reassured?
  - Do you want to impart confidence that they can maneuver effectively through the change?

- If you are delivering a speech on climate change or a social justice issue:
  - Do you want your listeners to feel optimistic and willing to make a difference?
- If you are speaking about a fundraising campaign:
  - Do you want your audience to feel excited about what those funds will pay for?
  - Do you want them to feel that your organization's work is enough of a priority that they will write out a check to support you?

When I did a virtual training for a team of construction engineers, I decided that what I wanted them to do was to make significant and noticeable improvements to their virtual presentation style. One team member followed up to show me how he had changed his background, lighting, and camera angle. The clarity underlying my call to action made this possible.

## Key Question 4: "What is the one thing I want my listeners to remember?"

As your listeners depart and go about their day, what's the one message you want them to take away? This is your **core message**.

Your core message is not the same thing as the topic of your speech. The topic is more like a working title; it just tells you generally what the speech is about. The core message connects to the needs of your audience and the purpose of this particular speech.

Here's an example. Over the years, I have given a multitude of different speeches about how to craft a speech (topic), depending on what I wanted my audience to learn and remember (core message). In the speech I mentioned above, my core message evolved from "This is how you give a speech" to "Learning speechmaking techniques will improve all communication, improve your confidence, and, therefore, gain you respect and authority in your company."

Your core message is the spinal cord of your speech, the structure that unifies your speech from beginning to end. It's the focus and source of the speech's energy, the essential idea that matters most.

You've identified the benefit to your listeners, what their needs are, and what you want them to do as a result of hearing your speech. Now you need to put your core message into words. Your answer to the question "What's the one thing I want my listeners to remember?" will help you zero in on it. Here are a couple of methods:

*Option 1*

Stand up, in your office or living room, and pretend there's an attentive audience listening to you. You've reached the end of your speech. Now, say this out loud: "If you remember only one thing from tonight's speech, it is: _____ _____."

If your core message spills out immediately, with ease and clarity, lucky you! Write it down. If it doesn't, keep talking out loud. Three times, four times, more if you need to.

Are you standing up, or did you skip that part? If you're still sitting down, get on your feet. Walk back and forth. Repeat the sentence. Keep talking. Keep walking.

Write down any key words that show up, images, phrases, or metaphors that you feel have energy. Hear what you say and put it on paper.

This process of creative discovery allows your ideas to emerge without overthinking. Eventually, your core message will reveal itself: your number one priority, the central idea you want your audience to remember.

**Option 2**

Ask yourself these questions:

- What am I passionate about and want to share with others?
- What problem do I know how to solve?
- What insights do I have that could help my listeners?
- How can my perspective change the world?
- What does this organization or team need to hear?
- What results have I delivered?

Don't sweat it if your core message doesn't come immediately—it takes some percolating before the coffee arrives. Once you find it, you will still have many choices to make. But as long as everything you include aligns directly to your core message, your speech will be focused and streamlined.

Here are some great examples of topics honed into core messages. All are an invitation to the audience to expand their thinking on the topic.

"People that society once considered disabled can now become the architects of their own identities and indeed continue to change those identities, by designing their bodies from a place of empowerment."

— Aimee Mullins, "My 12 Pairs of Legs," TED 2014


"I saw the capacity to reimagine my community buildings as an extension of my artistic practice. And with other creatives—architects, engineers, real estate finance people—together we might be able to think in more complicated ways about the reshaping of cities."

— Theaster Gates, "How to Revive a Neighborhood: With Imagination, Beauty, and Art," TED 2015


"Being cured is not where the work of healing ends. It's where it begins."

— Suleika Jaouad, "What Almost Dying Taught Me About Living," TED 2019


"Simply moving your body has immediate, long-lasting and protective benefits for your brain. And that can last for the rest of your life."

— Wendy Suzuki, "The Brain-Changing Benefits of Exercise," TED Women 2017

"Experiences of the self and of the world turn out to be kinds of controlled hallucinations, brain-based best guesses that remain tied to the world and the body in ways determined not by their accuracy but by their utility, by their usefulness for the organism in the business of staying alive."

— ANIL SETH, "HOW YOUR BRAIN INVENTS YOUR 'SELF'," TED MEMBERSHIP, 2021

Once you've found your core message, move on to the remaining three key questions.

## Key Question 5: "What do my listeners need to know?"

You have a core message, tailored to your listeners and leading to a call to action (what you want them to do, feel, or believe). But they won't act on your call to action just because you think it's a good idea. You need *them* to think it's a good idea.

So, now you must ask yourself, "What do my listeners need to know in order to understand my core message, connect with it, and feel inspired to act on it?"

Possibly you are introducing a new concept or theory. Almost certainly there is some information you need to impart, something you want them to learn. But it is well known that people don't make decisions based on logic. We make decisions based on how we feel. So, as important as it is for your speech to contain a logical, fact-based argument supporting your core message, it's just as important for it to generate emotion in your listeners.

And there are two other considerations:

1. Your listeners must understand you are not asking them to do something you haven't already done or would be prepared to do. For example, if you're speaking about the benefits of exercise, you'll want to share personal challenges you faced and actions you took in changing your own exercise habits. This gives your "ask" credibility when you ask others to join you.

2. Your listeners must feel that it is possible for them to get the results you are offering by acting on your call to action. In other words, they must feel empowered in the possibility that they can improve their lives, business, team, organization, or community.

Your answer to the question "What do my listeners need to know?" will probably be a combination of different kinds of information: personal stories, anecdotes, data, or logical argument. As you develop your speech, you will distill this information into your **key points**.

We'll discuss key points in detail later. For now, it's enough to identify what this particular audience needs to know in order to feel adequately informed and inspired to act on your call to action.

### Key Question 6: "Why me?"

Your listeners want to feel that you're worth listening to. They want to know they can trust you. So, what credentials do you bring?

Credentials can include the obvious: education, career history, leadership roles. Some audiences need to know that you have a masters in subject A or a long career in profession B. It's usually pretty clear when those are the right credentials to cite. But let's look a little further for ways to introduce yourself that will create rapport and trust.

You may have years of training and expertise, decades of study, a boatload of degrees or certifications—or your authority may rest simply on intense personal experience. You can establish your authority by recounting:

- how you came to be curious about your subject, and how you learned about it
- how a personal failure in the subject matter of your speech led you to a new idea
- how you learned about your subject through your upbringing, family, and/or cultural traditions
- how a client or customer overcame an obstacle, or experienced a great success, because of what you offer
- how the material you'll share in your speech changed your life

Different topics require different credentials. If you don't have the traditional credentials for your particular topic, you will need to establish why *your* credentials make you worthy of your listeners' attention. Be forthright. Claim your validity as a speaker on your topic, even if—especially if—it rests on credentials that are unconventional or surprising.

### Key Question 7: "How much time do I have?"

The time limit represents an agreement. An organization, your boss, or the event schedule gives you an allotted space for your speech. You honor that agreement by being 100% committed to its criteria.

If you haven't been given a specific time limit, don't take this as an invitation to go on for as long as you want. Agree with the person organizing the event, or the other speakers, how long your speech will be.

The potential consequences for going over time are:

- motivating your audience to keep checking the time
- prompting your audience to listen for cues that you're about to finish, rather than to the message in your words
- reducing the time available for speakers coming after you
- ruining future relationships and potential referrals
- seeming self-important and greedy for the spotlight

---

*Tip: Never exceed your allotted time*

---

Going over time is a common mistake, which people make for a variety of reasons. They may:

- believe everything they know on the subject must be shared
- neglect to prepare, and venture off on tangents and long-winded stories
- get carried away by enthusiasm and abandon their plan
- consider the amount of time given is a suggestion rather than a firm limit
- not account for potential delays, such as laughter or a drawn-out introduction

- not know the speed at which they speak

Jordan was excited about an upcoming presentation to potential clients and asked me to help. The topic, "Our conscious and unconscious relationship to money," was rich, intriguing, and personally relevant to everyone. Jordan had distilled it into a strong core message: "To have a healthy and positive relationship with money requires that you explore and examine the messages of your ancestors, primary family, and social stigmas."

He had 20 minutes. But as he ran his very powerful speech for me, he was barely one-third of the way through when the timer went off. And that was without the audience participation he had cleverly worked in.

We started calculating. Audience participation: 5 minutes. Q&A: 5 minutes. That left 10 minutes for the actual speech. So, not just two-thirds, but five-sixths of the draft speech would have to go!

We'll discuss audience participation and Q & A in more depth soon. If you're planning to include these features, you'll need an accurate estimate of the time they'll take. Don't cheat and reckon you'll finish the Q & A in 2 minutes. You won't. You'll run over time.

After you've made all the necessary subtractions, you'll have a length for your actual speech rather than for your presentation as a whole. You don't want to do what Jordan did and work hard composing a speech six times longer than your allotted time.

---

*Tip: Calculate a target length before you start composing your speech*

Speechminutes.com advises that a 20-minute speech is approximately 2,600 words. Approximately! Your results will vary. You have a natural pace and rhythm, which may be slower or faster than those of the folks at Speechminutes.com. Individual speakers can vary 20% or more in either direction.

So, find out where you fall on this spectrum. Choose a bit of text whose length you know—say, 500 words—and time yourself as you read it aloud at a pace that feels natural. Let's say 500 words took you 5 minutes. So if you have 12 minutes for your speech, you're aiming for around 1,200 words.

If this seems way shorter than you were expecting, don't fudge it. Don't figure on speaking more quickly! You may manage to say more of what you want to say, but it will be totally counterproductive. You'll lose your audience after a few seconds if you're speaking at warp speed.

Also, bear in mind that your actual speech will take longer than this rough calculation, since you'll be speaking to an audience rather than reading, and there may be interruptions of various kinds. The best strategy is to prepare a speech that's shorter than the time you have. If you have 20 minutes, craft a speech that should take you 15–17 minutes to deliver. If you have 10 minutes, craft one that you believe will take approximately 8.

Finishing early is not a problem, unless you're a long way short. A group expecting a 20-minute speech will feel cheated if you only give them 10. However, finishing 5 minutes early might provide a welcome breathing space. You can always fill up the time with an impromptu Q & A.

Once you've answered the seven key questions, you've developed the foundation of your speech. You have a core message. You know who your listeners are and what you want them to do, feel, or believe. You have articulated why they should listen to you. And you have an idea of how long your speech should be.

The next step is to gather your material and start composing your speech.

# 2

# Compose Your Speech

The start of a creative endeavor can feel barren. You know you've got something to say, something to share, something to contribute. But your mind is blank—or perhaps only thinly populated by a loose collection of thoughts.

This may be where you are right now. Or, you may be in the opposite place: your brain filled to the brim with ideas and content, all whirling and jostling for priority. There's brilliance in there, but right now it feels like a hurricane's passing through.

Either way, it's time to start selecting the material that will support your core message, and discarding the material that won't.

## Gather Your Treasures

The first step in arranging your content is to gather your treasures—all the material you might want to use in your speech. These could be personal stories, anecdotes, quotes, arguments, data, case studies, even jokes.

A good speech incorporates many different types of material, in order to reach the widest swath of listeners. Listeners who think logically and respect data will respond to models, statistics, and case studies. Listeners who approach things intuitively and creatively will respond to quotes, metaphors, and stories. A variety of material allows you to unpack and embellish your core message through multiple expressive and learning modalities.

This is what I call "full-spectrum speaking."

Here are some prompts to help you gather your treasures. Write each treasure down or make a note of where to find it. Sticky notes or index cards can be helpful, because you can easily color-code your treasures and rearrange the order.

- Collect stories: your own or those of family, clients and others that illustrate your core message.

- Find case studies that will back up specific points you want to make.

- List lived experiences (your own or other people's) that shed light on your core message.

- Find statistics or data that clarify and validate your key points.

- Collect quotes that distill or expand your core message.

You won't end up using all of the treasures you collect, but providing yourself with more than you need will give you inspiration and allow you to choose the treasure that best fits the purpose—whether for your opening, a key point, or your closing.

## Start Writing Your Speech

I find that most people start writing their speech in one of two ways: either they dive in and generate material which they'll organize later, or they make an outline which they'll fill in later.

Either method works fine. You may already know which suits you best. If not, experiment. Some people work best by trusting their creativity; others feel scattered and confused without a template to follow. Some "left-brain" people aren't comfortable if they don't have a road map, whereas others need to get out of their critical, analytical mind in order to go anywhere at all.

The first two methods below are for those who want to start by generating material. The third is for those who prefer to start with organization.

## Splat it

One of my clients described splatting as like throwing paint at a wall—allowing your ideas to flow freely without looking for logic or connections.

Sit down at your computer, or curl up in a chair with pen and paper. Put your thoughts into words without editing, critiquing, rewriting, or tossing anything out. All you're after here is raw material.

The big advantage of this method is that you aren't constrained: your options are wide open. Shut your inner critic away in a box; no matter how loud it shouts, don't listen. Anything that pops into your head is worth writing down. Once ideas start flowing, new ones bubble up from who knows where and surprise you.

You will end up with a plethora of material that will need to be organized and cut down. You can do that later. Most likely, scattered in your splat will be rough-cut gems—powerful words and phrases, ideas you want to share. The gems you find here, honed and polished, will be the highlights of your speech.

## Speak it

Good speakers don't read from a script. Public speaking is an oral art form, and this method gives you the opportunity to find your voice from the very start. Use an app on your phone to record yourself as you throw out phrases and ideas. You can stand and pretend you're delivering the speech. Better yet, pace back and forth. Many people find that physical movement helps the ideas flow. If you're one of those people who get their best ideas while driving, this may be a good technique for you.

Like splatting, this approach sidelines your inner critic. It also means you never have to face a blank page. I find that it frees me up, since I don't feel the pressure that most people feel when they sit down to write: to write something good. Feeling that you're supposed to write something good straight out of the gate is what makes many people give up. (And guess what? Most professional writers don't write their final draft first time out. They just get something down on paper and edit it later.)

So, walk back and forth. Say a few words. Keep moving, keep talking. It doesn't matter where you start—and you may get better results by deliberately *not* starting at the beginning. Say your core message aloud, with passion and commitment. Say your call to action. Repeat them and let other words build around them.

Allow your stream of consciousness to flow. You'll feel which phrases have energy and pop. Repeat those phrases, and see where the flow of your speaking takes you. You'll surprise yourself with moments of brilliance.

If you don't believe me, try it for yourself.

A further advantage of this technique is that your speech will never sound academic, overly formal, or unnatural. By starting with your unfiltered ideas and spontaneously generated words, you are capturing your most authentic voice. Plus, you're rehearsing your speech while you're composing it. So, when you deliver it for real, you will be fully connected to every word—which is what makes a speech powerful, moving, and memorable.

When you feel that you've reached a natural stopping point, transcribe the recording. Once it's down on paper, you can manipulate, add, alter, and expand your ideas.

I repeat this process multiple times while developing a speech.

*Marshal your material*

Now you'll need to make sense of all this material. Grab some more sticky notes or index cards. Listen to your voice recording or read your splat. When you notice an idea with energy, a catchy turn of phrase, a strong insight or line of argument, maybe a joke that will pull your audience in, write it on a sticky note or card and put it on your wall or idea board. You'll start to see where ideas and phrases connect up, where stories or examples develop your argument, where images and moments of true emotion will bring your speech to life.

## Map it

I'm an avid list-maker, a skill (or obsession) I learned from my mother. My errand list is numbered so that I can follow a route with maximum gas- and time-saving benefits. Like my errand list, a speech template orders your material so that you travel most efficiently from one point to the next. You may find that making a template of your speech is the way to maximize your energy- and time-saving benefits.

Years ago, I hired a speaking coach. Before I sent her my content, she emailed me a template to follow. At the time, the idea of writing my content into the spaces in her template completely turned me off. But even though it's not my preferred method (despite my errand lists), I find that it can be extremely helpful to my clients, such as Daniel, a musician I met at a group training, who said that my "customized map" approach was exactly what he needed to focus his thoughts.

Even if you began writing your speech by splatting or speaking it, the customized map will help you rehearse it. I'll discuss how to create your customized map in chapter 6. Before we get there, we need to understand the overall flow of a speech, how it leads its listeners from introduction to content to call to action.

# 3

## Shape Your Speech

Imagine, for a moment, you are the listener rather than the speaker. What will make you feel comfortable, excited about what you're learning, and inspired to act?

Listening to an effective speech is like walking through a museum. First, you enter the lobby. It's a vast, open space. There are some large, eye-catching displays (maybe a dinosaur skeleton or an enormous sculpture), but you probably don't look at them closely: they just indicate what kind of museum this is. They set the context and invite you to make your first connection to the subject matter you're about to explore. You know you are entering a space that will inform and inspire you; the prevailing emotion is anticipation. It's a welcoming space, and a map is provided, which you glance at but don't have to study closely.

Now, you go into specific rooms. Let's say you have an audio guide leading you from exhibit to exhibit. Probably the guide doesn't direct your attention to every single item on display: that would overwhelm you. (Just as in your speech, you don't want to overload your listeners with too much information.) The guide ushers you along a path that gives you the highlights of what the museum offers—and, perhaps, intrigues you enough to want to come back and see more.

Once you've made your way through the exhibits, you exit through the gift shop. This is the museum's equivalent of a call to action: Buy our merchandise! Support our mission!

Every speech—like every museum—is different. You will compose yours according to its unique combination of subject matter, audience, event, and purpose. But all good speeches—like all good museums—have a natural flow. They also have a natural shape, which we will now explore.

## The Speechwriter's Hourglass

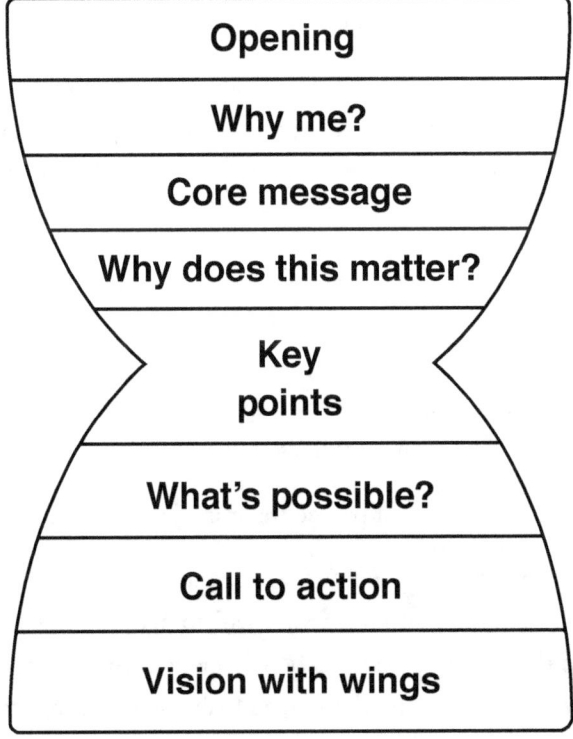

Imagine your speech laid out on the ground, from top (beginning) to bottom (end). The width represents the broadness or specificity of the ideas you're expressing. When the shape is wide, the focus is broad. When the shape is narrow, the focus is specific.

The top of the hourglass represents your opening. You're introducing your audience to the topic of your speech without saying baldly and boringly, "I'm going to speak to you about . . ." The opening:

- captures the big picture

- offers an entrance point that awakens awe
  and anticipation in your audience

- sets the context for your speech

We'll explore various methods for achieving this below.

From this broad opening, your speech begins to narrow into specifics, giving your core message focus and clarity. In the narrow section, you might include:

- details of a problem or its solution

- data or statistics

- stories that demonstrate the impact of
  your topic on individual lives

- the nuts and bolts of procedure or implementation

These are your key points: what your listeners need to know in order to get on board with your call to action. Now that you've equipped them with the necessary information, you can start moving them toward application. The shape of your speech starts to broaden again as you move back to a wider perspective: the possibility of implementing the vision you've set out, and fueling it with inspiration. In fact, you're painting an even broader picture than the one you painted at the beginning: this is a picture of the world as it would be if your core message is heeded and acted upon. I call this section **a vision with wings**.

## The Basic Building Blocks of a Speech

I find it helpful to break down the parts of a speech, and the kind of material you'll be using, into specific categories. I call them building blocks.

The order I've laid out below is a basic sequence, but it isn't set in stone. Feel free to choose from among these structural building blocks and order them in the way that best serves your purpose, your style, and the specific requirements of your speech.

We'll discuss the content building blocks that you will use to fill out this sequence—such as story, quotes, and data—in the next chapter.

### Basic Building Block 1: Opening

Imagine you're attending a theater performance. You purchase your ticket and find your seat. As you peruse the program, the house lights dim and the murmur of conversation stops. As the auditorium goes dark, the stage curtains open. You can almost touch the collective anticipation. You, and everyone else in the audience, are ready for whatever the production will give you.

Now, imagine yourself giving your speech. Your audience feels that same anticipation. They are there to hear you speak, and they are ready to be engaged by what you say. Even if they're there unwillingly, or simply waiting for the next speaker, they have made a mental agreement to give you their attention if you merit it. You don't have to fight for their attention. What you must do is seize it, hold it—and intensify it.

> "Your opening needs to be a kind of pleasant shock therapy. It should grab people."
> — PRIYA PARKER, AUTHOR OF
> THE ART OF GATHERING

Your audience is expecting to be interested, entertained, informed, and/or motivated, and you want to let them know quickly that their expectations will be met—in spades! You're going to deliver on your promise.

A strong opening gives people a reason to listen right out of the gate. Why do people listen? Because what they're hearing surprises them, shocks them, makes them laugh, makes them recognize something of themselves in your words, or makes them feel you're talking directly, and relevantly, to them. To return to our earlier metaphor, you're meeting them on the shore of the lake of your ideas and inviting them in.

In your opening, you're answering the question in your listeners' minds: What is this speech about? But you're not going to open with: "Hello, this speech is about _____." Just as when you invite someone to your house for dinner, you don't just open the door and say, "There's the food."

Instead, you'll craft your opening for maximum attention-grabbing quality. You might choose a real-life story, or a quote, or a riveting statistic. You might ask your listeners a question that engages them in the search for an answer. Whatever kind of material you choose, the number one priority of your opening is to engage your listeners mentally and emotionally.

*Tip: Make a personal connection with your audience*

One of the best examples of making this connection is Sir Ken Robinson's TED Talk, "Do Schools Kill Creativity?" His tone is casual yet intimate as he offers a synopsis of what the attendees at this particular conference—himself included—have heard so far. In this short opening, he breaks down the wall between himself and his audience by referencing their shared experience.

He then builds a bridge from the themes of the conference to the ideas he will be setting forth in his speech, and arrives at a statement of his core message: "Creativity is as important in education as literacy and we should treat it with the same status." Owing to the connection he has established with his listeners, that message lands with impact and clarity.

Robinson chose an easy, conversational style, which may not be appropriate for your speech. Some situations require a bolder opening or a more formal approach. Your answer to Key Question 2, "Who are my listeners?," will give you insight into your best approach to your opening.

Kamala knew who her audience would be: young, environmentally aware, and invested in the community she was speaking about because they lived there. She opened by asking the audience a personal question that took them back to their childhood. This not only engaged them emotionally but focused them on her topic: trees.

"When you were a child, did you have a favorite tree? Was it a place to hide? To climb? A safe haven or a secret friend no one else knew you had?

I had one too. It was small and the bark was smooth. All summer ladybugs would swarm the branches and I was just tall enough to lift myself on the lowest branch and climb up to watch for hours.

As a country and as citizens, we've stopped saying 'Thank you' to our trees."

A personal story can also make for a strong, welcoming opening, as it invites the audience to share the speaker's lived experience. Susan Cain's TED Talk, "The Power of Introverts," opens with a humorous anecdote: Cain, as a child, packing a suitcase full of books for her first time at summer camp. This made sense to her, she explains, because in her family reading was "a primary group activity." She expands on the vision she had of a book-reading camp, and the confusion and disappointment she felt when the vision didn't come true. This story perfectly encapsulates Cain's topic: society's unrealistic, even damaging expectation that people should be extroverted. It sets us up for her core message: "Introverts bring extraordinary talents and abilities to the world, and should be encouraged and celebrated."

A strong opening might:

- refer to the experience of your listeners, as Sir Ken Robinson did

- offer a compelling or shocking statistic

- recount a story: a personal experience, a story about someone you know, a historical anecdote, or a myth or fable. The story need not be humorous, but it must have emotional content.

- call for audience participation by asking a yes-or-no question: "By raise of hands, how many of you . . ."

- invite the audience to put themselves in a scenario by using the word "imagine": "Imagine you are . . ."

- present a quote that crystallizes your big idea

**Weak openings**

A weak opening makes your listeners wonder and wander. They wonder if you are really going to deliver, and their attention wanders. Maybe they even question your credibility or preparedness.

Here are some examples of weak openings:

**1. "Thank you, thank you . . ."**

You've probably heard a speaker spend the first few minutes thanking everyone: the audience, the sponsors, the person who introduced them. There's nothing wrong with gratitude and appreciation—except at the beginning of a speech. A humdrum opening lets the sense of anticipation dissipate. The energy level in the room drops fast.

Think back, if you can, to the last time you heard a speaker start this way. Did they succeed in ramping the excitement back up? My guess is no. For two reasons: one, because it's an uphill struggle after such a start—the speaker would have had to put in extra effort to regain the audience's interest. And two: because a speaker who starts unfocused tends to stay unfocused. A weak opening is often a symptom of a weak speech.

However, maybe you're concerned about seeming ungrateful. You might be asking, "Where can I express my gratitude for my host?"

Tracey asked me to help her design a keynote speech for the Western Women Business Center Conference. When we started, she was opening with "Good morning and thank you . . . thank you." With a little urging, we developed a stronger start:

> "'Women at the Table' is a powerful statement—the recognition of the collective power, wisdom, and vision of women from diverse backgrounds. It's a call to action."

She followed this by expressing her gratitude to Western Women Business Center for the invitation to speak.

**2. "My name is . . ."**

Usually followed by, "I am the [job title] of [name of company]. I'm here to talk to you about [topic of speech]."

Chances are that everybody knows this already. They've read the program, or the signage in the lobby, or the memo that instructed them to be here. So this speaker's first words are telling the audience something they already know. Since the opening serves as a promise for the rest of the speech, the subliminal message is that the audience doesn't actually have to listen since they'll just be told things they already know, or things are obvious and uninteresting. I guarantee you that one person is already checking the time. At least a few more are planning dinner.

**3. Wake me up when this is over**

Example 1: "I am here today to talk to you a little bit about project management. Specifically, about why project management is important for you. You all have projects that are currently in flight or about to start. What if I told you that without project management it is very difficult to hit the true value against the business opportunity for that project. You all have strategic goals and every initiative you start advances those goals. Project management ensures that the goals of the project closely align with the strategic goals of the division. Here are three other reasons why project management is important . . ."

Example 2: "Hi! I'm Piper from Aroma Essences. I want to thank you for giving me the opportunity to tell you about myself and my work. I am a nationally certified clinical aromatherapist with over 500 hours of education. I have additional trainings in PMADs, which are perinatal mood and anxiety disorders (such as postpartum depression) and treating trauma. I have been working with and studying natural health practices for over two decades. My mission is to help others get to the root, the origin of what is negatively impacting their quality of life so that profound healing can occur."

In the first example, the speaker uses industry jargon and vague and unfinished ideas. In the second example, time and audience attention are wasted as the speaker shares unnecessary information.

*Tip: First orientate your listeners in your topic, then weave in your expertise*

**4. The tidal wave opening**

"As an information security officer in my current IT job, I would tell you there is zero percent unemployment for IT security professionals. Hopefully, that gets your attention and I can offer you some thoughts on a path towards an IT security career. There are several big reasons why the demand is so high for IT security professionals. First, the rapid changes in the world related to the internet and other technologies create new security challenges every month. Second, higher education in general is struggling to graduate students qualified to fill these jobs. And third, the wide breadth of specialties that are covered by this field."

Does this deluge of information leave you flailing for something to hold on to? It did me.

**5. The joke that falls flat**

I attended an event where a male speaker, third or fourth on the program, began by making a joke about being between two women. To make things worse, the audience was predominantly female. Nobody laughed. This speaker shot himself in the foot before he even started.

## Basic Building Block 2: Why me?

```
┌─────────────────┐
│     Opening     │
├─────────────────┤
│     Why me?     │
└─────────────────┘
```

You've captivated your audience with a compelling opening. Now what? This is a good time to establish your credibility and authority, so that your listeners feel that what you say will be worth the investment of their attention.

If you are going to be introduced before you begin speaking, by a host or colleague or event sponsor, you might choose to bypass this building block, since that introduction should include your credentials. (You know this will happen, because you've provided them with your short bio ahead of time.) However, there may be more personal credentials to add: how you came to this topic, or why it matters to you. Refer to you answer to Key Question 6, "Why me?"

When deciding how much to say about yourself, follow this advice from Chris Anderson, TED curator: "Remember that the purpose of your talk is to gift an idea, not to self-promote." So, keep the information about yourself to the minimum required to convince your audience that you're worth listening to.

## Basic Building Block 3: Core message

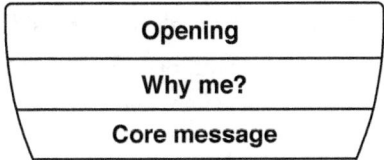

Having set the context and given your credentials, you'll move from the big picture to your core message. If your speech was a film scene, this would be a zoom in: focusing the audience's attention on what's most important in the scene.

As we've discussed, your core message is a clear articulation of why the topic of your speech matters. It encapsulates a benefit for your listeners or a vision of a better world. It is the answer to Key Question 4, "What's the one thing I want my listeners to remember?" Now we'll examine how to weave it into your speech.

These are the most effective techniques:

**1. Phrase your core message as a declaration**

A 50-million-dollar architectural project for an art museum in Montana was on the line. Alan and Devon reached out to me to improve their pitch to the selection committee. The first version gives information about their team, but it's indirect and doesn't fully express the strength, skills, and benefits they bring to the table. With a bit of exploration, we came up with the improved version. Strong phrasing and key words highlight the reasons why the committee should hire their practice.

*Pre-conviction*

"Ours is a blended team. As we talked about in our first meeting, we think diversity is important. Whether you're talking about ecosystems or financial portfolios, diversity is crucial for success. It was certainly a key consideration when putting together the best team for your project."

*With conviction*

"You are looking to create a building for the future. You are envisioning a space to engage your audience and invite new members to your organization. To meet your vision, we've put together an outstanding team that

- is forward-thinking
- has design expertise
- and has the keen ability to listen to you and transform your vision into reality.

A team that:

- brings community and fundraising knowledge and experience to the table
- and that knows the community's character, traditions, and value. We speak the language of this town."

If you find that your first draft is wishy-washy, you may not be hitting the bull's-eye of your message. Here, the message changed from "Our team is great because it's blended and diversity is important" to "Our team is strong and perfect for this job and here's why."

Most importantly, make sure your core message speaks to your own deepest convictions. When you say something that you believe in the depth of your heart, confidence and believability will resonate in your voice and your message.

Here's how Susan Cain states her core message in "The Power of Introverts":

"I got the message that somehow my quiet and introverted style of being was not necessarily the right way to go, that I should be trying to pass as more of an extrovert. And I always sensed deep down that this was wrong and that introverts were pretty excellent just as they were . . . Now, this is what many introverts do, and it's our loss for sure, but it is also our colleagues' loss and our communities' loss and, at the risk of sounding grandiose, it is the world's loss because **when it comes to creativity and leadership, we need introverts doing what they do best.**"

She continues to unpack this central idea: how the abilities and talents of introverts should be respected, valued, and celebrated.

### 2. Express your core message as a vision of the future

Many speakers have a dynamic vision of the change they'd like to bring about, the world they'd like to see. Their talk is an invitation to the audience to share that vision. A great example of this is Sir Ken Robinson's "Do Schools Kill Creativity?" Here's how he delivered his core message:

"I want to talk about education and I want to talk about creativity. [Great! Now we, the audience, know exactly what his topic is.] My contention is that **creativity now is as important in education as literacy, and we should treat it with the same status.**"

Immediately, his audience began to applaud. He had them from very soon after hello. Jokingly, he ad-libbed, "Okay, now we can go home!" That would make public speaking so much easier! But you and I know there's much more to share.

### 3. Phrase your core message as a question

Questions evoke curiosity. A core message expressed as a question cues the audience to focus their attention on the answer that follows. Here's an example from Arnav Kapur's 2019 TED Talk, "How AI Could Become an Extension of Your Mind." He has introduced his desire to "integrate human and machine intelligence right inside our own bodies, to augment us instead of diminishing or replacing us." He follows this up with two questions:

> "Could we combine what people do best, such as creative and intuitive thinking, with what computers do best, such as processing information and perfectly memorizing stuff? Could this whole be better than the sum of its parts?"

Another technique is to use your opening to cue your listeners how to answer the question that holds your core message. This makes them feel that they are arriving at an understanding of your subject under their own steam—in other words, to return to our earlier image of the lake, you've made them feel so comfortable that they're ready to dive right in. In his TED Talk "Are We in Control of Our Own Decisions?", Dan Ariely opens with a couple of impossible-to-reverse visual illusions and then asks:

> "If we have these predictable, repeatable mistakes in vision, which we're so good at, what's the chance that we don't make even more mistakes in something we're not as good at?"

—such as financial decision-making. The audience laughs, because they recognize they've made those mistakes in their own lives. They're ready to accept his evidence that much of our everyday decision-making is also subject to illusion.

## Basic Building Block 4: Why does this matter?

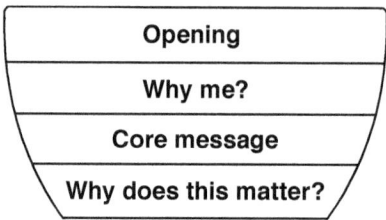

Steven Cohen, a speaking consultant, wrote, "Audiences start out listening to speeches by asking, 'Why should I care?' That's the speaker's job: to take the audience from 'why' to 'how.' But first you have to answer 'why.'"

---

*Tip: Highlight the benefit to your audience as early as possible. Help them see where they are and where they could be.*

---

In the past, audiences expected speakers essentially to give them a lecture, imparting wisdom and knowledge unto them. That was the norm. Today, with information and knowledge readily accessible online, we expect more. Audiences want to feel you are speaking with them, not at them. They demand a sense of engagement and connection. They demand that your speech is relevant to their lives.

To be relevant, you must know what matters to your audience. This is why knowing your audience is key. Here are some ways to let your audience know you are thinking about them:

• Address issues your listeners are currently facing.

- Acknowledge your awareness of their experience by saying things like "I get it" and "I know you'd rather be . . ."

- Discuss what opportunities they could gain or lose.

- Use inclusive language.

These are the questions your listeners will be asking themselves:

- Why does the topic of this speech matter to my business or personal life?

- In what ways can the core message of this speech make a difference?

- If we don't follow the recommendations of this speaker, what will be jeopardized?

- How will I, my community or organization benefit from this speaker's core message?

Your answers to Key Question 3, "What do you want your listeners to do, feel, or believe?," and Key Question 1, in which you considered your listeners' motivation, provide the material for this building block. Connect with your listeners' sense of meaning, and they will carry your message forward into their future decisions, actions, and maybe even beliefs.

Many speakers introduce a "problem" in this building block, and go on to unpack the reasons why the system, method, procedure, belief, approach, or idea no longer serves the community or business or isn't providing the desired results. By clarifying what's broken, they're setting up the audience for the solution they'll provide later on, in the call to action.

## Basic Building Block 5: Key points

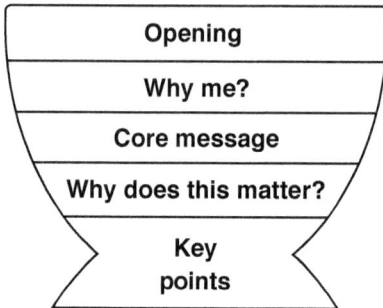

By the time your speech narrows into the neck of the hourglass, you are discussing the concrete details of your subject. This is the nuts and bolts of your speech.

If you stated a problem, this is where you demonstrate what's wrong. If you're introducing a new system, this is where you explain its components or the steps in using it. If you introduced a vision of the future, this is where you offer clear details of what that vision is.

The information in your key points should be concrete, palpable. Your audience can see it, hear it, know what it feels like. Specific information anchors your message into your listeners' own personal experiences of the world.

Let's look again at Susan Cain's "The Power of Introverts." In this section of her speech, she:

- defines introversion.

- gives examples of how our classrooms and workplaces are designed for constant interaction.

- demonstrates that introverts can be powerful, outspoken leaders, by listing the examples of Eleanor Roosevelt, Rosa Parks, and Mahatma Gandhi.

Every topic suggests a vast amount of concrete information to choose from. How do you choose what to include? A common complaint from audiences is that speakers give too much information. You don't want to come across as verbose or showoffy, and you don't want to overwhelm your listeners with a plethora of facts and figures. You want to include just enough to make your point powerfully, and no more.

### The Rule of Three

Limiting your argument to three main points offers benefits to both you and your audience. It forces you to choose your most powerful ammunition and allows you to deliver it with maximum impact. And it simplifies things for your listeners, making it easier for them to absorb and remember the information you give them, thereby making it more likely that they will act on it.

---

*Tip: Keep it simple*

---

We'll discuss later how to give these three points maximum impact, by supporting them with story, data, and examples. The task now is to clarify what they are.

Your answer to Key Question 5, "What does my audience need to know?," gives you the basis for your key points. Now is the time to streamline that material and make it user-friendly. Hone it down to the three most pertinent points. If you only have one or two key points, that is perfectly acceptable—especially if your speech is short.

You probably had a sense of which were the most important points when you answered Key Question 5. But now that your speech is starting to take shape, look at them again. Do you still feel that those are the strongest and most essential pieces of information in conveying your core message to this particular audience? Or, given the opening you've chosen, does one of your other points resonate with it more powerfully?

**"If I don't tell them everything..."**
I hear this from clients all the time. "If I don't tell them everything, they won't understand!"

Evan came to me after being accepted as a speaker at TEDx Asheville in 2019. This was his core message:

> "Veganism is an incredibly powerful strategy for sustainability—the possibility that human and other life will flourish on the planet forever."

As you can tell from this snippet, Evan was passionate about his subject. He was convinced that he had to share every benefit of veganism, and every reason for his devoted commitment to it: how he became a vegan, its potential to ameliorate climate change, its contribution to sustainability, its health benefits, animal rights, all supported with data displayed on multiple slides. If any one of these components was omitted, he believed, his audience would leave without a full understanding of why veganism has the potential to change the world for the better.

He had 18 minutes to speak.

Evan, an academic, was hardwired to teach. I explained to him that in this setting, his job as a speaker was not to teach but simply to ignite curiosity. It would be impossible to convey the entire scope of his subject in 18 minutes, and cramming in the information would only send his audience racing to the refreshment bar.

*Tip: Ignite your listeners' curiosity instead of trying to tell them everything*

A curious audience wants to know more—and you will tell them how to find out more: by buying your book, visiting your website, or otherwise following up on the call to action you leave them with. It's far more effective to tell an audience less, but tell it with engagement and relevance to their lives, than to bludgeon them with facts and figures. An exhausted listener loses interest and stops paying attention, and will therefore be far less likely to heed your call to action.

The information you had to leave out in order to streamline your content can still be shared with your audience. Here are some ways to do that:

- Provide a handout with additional information

- Offer a follow-up session

- Invite your listeners to speak with you after the event

- Direct your listeners to your book, your website, or other sources of additional information

- Follow up your event with an email thanking your listeners for attending and including resources for continued exploration of your topic

### Basic Building Block 6: What's possible?

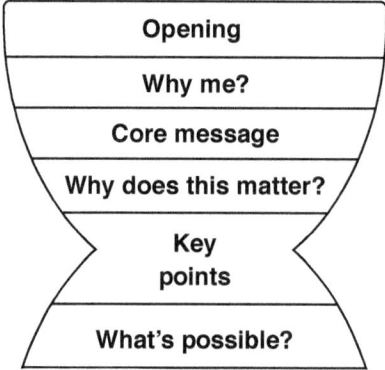

Now that your listeners know what you need them to know, you can take them to a consideration of what's possible—for our company, our community, for each individual person.

As I said earlier, the best way to make your core message stick is to let your listeners know why they should care. In this building block, you demonstrate how your ideas add benefit to your audience's personal or working lives, to an organization's strategic plan or proposal, or to the community at large.

The hourglass is widening again. You are pointing the way: presenting a possibility, and instilling in your audience a sense that what you are offering is genuinely possible—not just in the abstract but in their own lives.

> *"People are empowered not by that which they know is true, but rather by that which they believe is possible."*
> —Neil Gordon, speaking coach

Here is how Susan Cain marks this transition in "The Power of Introverts":

> "I am saying that the more freedom we give introverts to be themselves, the more likely they are to come up with their own unique solutions to these problems."

She is moving her listeners toward considering possible solutions to this societal bias, and giving them a vision of the benefits—not just to introverts, but to everyone—that this would bring.

As you do this, you may want to refer back to your key points, showing how they support your core message. By reviewing them, you anchor them clearly and succinctly in the minds of your listeners. My client Alex, a consultant to orthodontists' practices, took this approach:

> "By implementing these three team-building and client-centered practices into your day-to-day operation, you'll create greater job satisfaction for the office staff—and since you spend eight hours with these people every day, who wouldn't want more of that!
>
> With your improved face-to-face experiences with clients, loyalty and positive word-of-mouth recommendations will become very evident. Because of your willingness to implement a new strategy, you'll see increase of case acceptance. Now is the time to embark on steps toward greater personal and professional success."

And for another example, which leads beautifully into the next building block, let's circle back to Kamala's speech about environmental injustice. In this building block, she makes a strong appeal to her audience's emotions. Notice how she uses the techniques of repetition and contrast—what we don't want (referring back to her key points) versus what we stand for—to evoke urgency:

"We don't want a future where the voices of our communities are getting lost in order to favor an industrial agenda.

We don't want a future where loss of life is now more possible and prevalent than ever because we didn't value our forests for what they provide us.

We stand for the forests that can't plead their case.

We stand with communities who deserve the space to share their voices.

Stand with us!"

Kamala's language is both eloquent and commanding. This section of her speech gives impetus and momentum to what follows: the call to action.

### Basic Building Block 7: Call to action

Let's follow Kamala straight into her call to action:

"Go for a hike and remember all that nature provides and teaches us and all that we must continue to say thank you for.

Call your local representative and let them know that you don't want wood pellet biomass in your state or town."

Then, to underscore the power of community action, she begins her "vision with wings" with the word "Together," followed by an inspirational invitation to imagine a better world. We'll pick that up later.

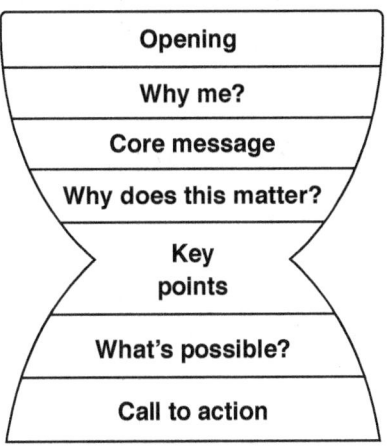

You've stated your core message passionately, broken it down into three key points so that your audience can grasp its importance, and shown how your message fits into the wider world. The call to action clarifies the ramifications of what you've proposed: what needs to be done, and how it might be done. Your call to action says, essentially, "Now that you understand and are moved by what I've told you, what actions can you take? Let me offer you one, two, or three." You probably want to limit your call to action to three items, as that's usually as many as most people can take in, though Bryan Stevenson, executive director of the Equal Justice Initiative, had four in his riveting speech "4 Rules for Achieving Peace and Justice."

If you have a call to action in your speech, your goal is for your listeners to heed it. Rarely do we know if a call to action was heard or acted upon—or when. An audience member might circle back to it six months later, when the issue becomes personal for them. What you can do is make sure your call to action is as clear and powerful as possible. Make it specific, so that your listeners understand clearly how to act on the inspiration your speech has given them.

---

*Tip: An effective call to action has an "ask"*

---

Look back at your answer to Key Question 3: "What do I want my listeners to do, feel, or believe?" That is the basis for your call to action.

Here is Susan Cain's call to action:

"Number one: Stop the madness for constant group work. Just stop it.

Okay, number two: Go to the wilderness. Be like Buddha, have your own revelations.

Number three: Take a good look at what's inside your own suitcase and why you put it there. So, extroverts, maybe your suitcases are also full of books. Or maybe they're full of champagne glasses or skydiving equipment. Whatever it is, I hope you take these things out every chance you get and grace us with your energy and your joy.

But introverts, you being you, you probably have the impulse to guard very carefully what's inside your own suitcase. And that's okay. But occasionally, just occasionally, I hope you will open up your suitcases for other people to see, because the world needs you and it needs the things you carry."

Do you see how her message is now moving forward with vision and purpose? She's sent it out into the world.

In 2018, at the Asheville Chamber of Commerce WomanUP Celebration event, I sat spellbound as futurist Rebecca Ryan gave the keynote speech. Titled "Fearless Integrity," its core message was "By paying attention to everyday moments, we have the opportunity to wake up, be present, and see the splendors of the world." Impelled by a recent cancer scare, Ryan spoke with passion and purpose, and her call to action had such powerful urgency that I couldn't help but act. As she suggested, I began to write down, each day, one thing I'd seen and one thing I'd heard. Not only did I follow this practice with increasing pleasure and awareness of its value, but it also motivated me to write several short inspirational stories.

**Clarifying your call to action**

As we just saw, Kamala built up to her call to action with a "What's Possible" building block taking her key points into contrasting visions of the future. If a "What's Possible" building block isn't appropriate for your speech, you may want to build up to your call to action with something else that prompts your listeners to heed it:

- "Three actions drastically changed my life. I offer them to you now."

- "Now that you understand _____, here are two actions you can take."

- "We have a responsibility to shift our focus and change our behaviors. We all have agency. Join me in _____."

- "Now that I've laid out our company's strategy for improving work conditions, I'm encouraging each of you to take one action to make this a success. The cumulative effect of multiple actions is what will make this change possible."

**Weak calls to action**

Perhaps your listeners are inspired by your core message but uncertain what exactly you want them to do. Or perhaps you haven't evoked enough emotion to make them want to expend the effort you're asking for. Or perhaps what you're asking is more about you than about them. You might even be asking the impossible.

**1. Noncommittal**

A theater company director came to me for advice on a speech she would give at the opening night of her season. Here is her call to action as it stood before we worked on it:

> "If you'd like to make your tax-deductible donation tonight, we take cash, check, or credit card. To make online donations, find out other ways you might get involved, or to learn more about our current season, please fill out the card in your playbill and leave it with us as you exit the theater this evening."

The very first word introduces the possibility that we don't want to support her! Of course, there are many reasons why we might not, but she herself has introduced the possibility that we simply may not feel compelled to. Though she has just told us about the groundbreaking work her company is doing, she seems uncertain about whether she's convinced us of its importance. She has not connected the body of her speech with her call to action.

Here's the improved version:

> "For us to bring this vision on stage, bring you and the Asheville community quality shows, and grow the infrastructure of the company, it will cost us $50,000 this year.
>
> If you believe in our mission to make theater that makes a difference through building community and facilitating awareness, and enjoy attending our performances and events, we invite you tonight to make your tax-deductible donation during intermission in the lobby."

Now her core message—"our company makes theater that makes a difference through building community and facilitating awareness"—is tied tightly to her call to action. Her appeal for donations taps into the audience's commitment to the arts, the community, and her company. She's also giving clear instructions about where and when the action can be taken—during intermission, in the lobby—without repeating information that's written on the card in the playbill, trusting that people have found it and can read it for themselves.

### 2. Unclear

Your listeners may be inspired to take action, but they don't understand exactly what they should do. Here's the unedited, unclear version:

"There are plenty of people in Buncombe County who have no idea that our children struggle to get access to the very basics of life: food and shelter. By joining Highlands Circle, you could give to someone that same experience that I had that day in our office—opening their eyes to what is happening and motivating them to act."

And here's the clarified version:

"Many in Buncombe County have no idea that our children struggle for basics of life: food and shelter. Highlands Circle is focused on educating others about our community and is looking for new members to contribute ideas and fresh energy to this effort. By joining Highlands Circle, you could give to someone the experience I had that day—opening their eyes to what is happening and motivating them to act.

If you're interested in taking the next step, please sign up on the sheet that I will be passing around. I would love to connect you with whichever one of our committees fits your passion best."

### 3. Overly demanding

From small children to wise elders, no one likes to be told what to do. If your call to action is overly demanding, you'll annoy your audience and send them marching in the opposite direction, or out the door. If you do want people to make a major change, get them started with a bite-sized invitation.

Let's say you're a farmer and your core message is "Growing your own food will enrich your life." Your call to action wouldn't be "Plow a plot of land and grow ten rows of corn." Nobody is going to do that from a standing start. Your call to action needs to be doable—something like, "Buy two pots, a bag of potting soil, a tomato plant and basil. Put them in the sun, water them, and you have the makings of a delicious salad all summer long."

You may have had the (unfortunately common) experience of being asked by a speaker to give up something you enjoy, make a drastic change, or adopt a new way of living. Your tendency was probably to resist. Evan, who gave the speech about the benefits of veganism, felt that he had to make that big ask. Instead of implying "You should …" in his demanding call to action, he found an open-ended and honest way to say it: "As should be apparent by now, I'm asking you all to adopt a vegan lifestyle and plant-based diet." Even if the call to action didn't convince his audience, his closing, which offered a heartfelt and altruistic vision of our future, inspired us at least to think about it.

> "With that, I leave you with a final thought. I want to see a future where humanity has halted the dual crises of climate change and biodiversity loss; a future where we live in peace with all life on earth; and a future where we love and care for not only our fellow humans, but our animal companions as well. If you share that vision with me, I invite you to embrace veganism as we cultivate a sustainable world together."

I call this kind of inspirational closing a vision with wings.

## Basic Building Block 8: Closing: Vision with wings

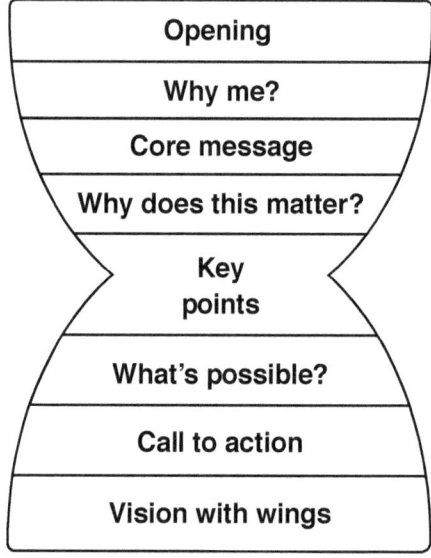

Having heard the bulk of your speech, your listeners are filled with ideas, new knowledge, and fresh perspective. Don't give them yet another thing to think about or understand! Instead, return to the essence of your core message and carry it with momentum from the present moment into the future.

An effective closing is a grab-you-by-the-throat and want-to-fly inspirational invocation. It's emotionally uplifting. An effective closing:

- helps your listeners see what's possible

- inspires confidence and motivates your listeners to accomplish your call to action

- provokes curiosity, making your listeners want to know more about your subject

- inspires your listeners to talk about your subject to others

And, as an added bonus, it:

- leaves your listeners feeling you are a respectable and motivating leader

Let's return to Kamala's speech one more time. In her closing, she circled back to her opening, about having a favorite tree:

> "Together we can ensure a better future where all children can continue to have special connections to the natural world. Where we insist on everyone's right to clean air and water. Where we can always have a favorite tree. Where we actually see the forest for the trees. And where we always say, Thank you."

Most people have, at some point in their lives, made an emotional connection with a tree. Sending our memories back to that moment directly connected each one of us with her core message and landed it squarely in our hearts. When she delivered this closing at my Speaker's Learning Lab, she received a standing ovation.

Here's another memorable example, from Susan Cain's "The Power of Introverts":

> "So, I wish you the best of all possible journeys, and the courage to speak softly."

Cain is using a powerful technique here, in saying "the courage to speak softly." This is a surprising combination of words, almost a contradiction, since we tend to associate courage with dramatic action—so it's arresting and memorable. Her closing speaks directly to her theme: though introverts are discounted by society because they don't speak up, being true to yourself is a virtue, worthy of admiration and praise.

**Weak closings**
I recently heard an architect give an inspiring 30-minute speech that discussed the rebuilding of communities that had been redlined in the 1960s and then razed for highways or new building. His firm is working on revitalization projects that involve members of the community retelling its history and the stories of the elders who were uprooted. He closed his presentation by saying, "I don't think I've gone over my time. If you have questions, I'll be in the lobby. Thank you."

Imagine how deflated the audience felt. The subliminal message was: "I'm done. I don't have any more slides, and I don't really know or care if my speech has had any impact on you. Now you can get on with your lives."

So, in your closing, **do not**:

• apologize if you've gone over your time.

  *Instead:* Finish strong and confident.

• apologize for any reason.

  *Instead:* Maintain composure, and don't attract attention to anything that was outside your control.

• say, "I hope you enjoyed the presentation."

  *Instead:* Assume that your listeners enjoyed it and were moved by it, and project that confidence.

- end with your contact information, such as website or location.

  *Instead:* Include this in the call to action and communicate it as a benefit to your listener. For example, "Many of the points we covered today are on my website. If you need a refresher, go to [URL]," or "If you want to learn more or stay in touch, sign up for my monthly newsletter. Pick up my information at my table in the lobby."

*(Note: If you've been invited by an organization to give this speech, check with them before promoting your business, such as by giving website or social media information. The organization may have policies concerning product or service promotion.)*

**Effective closings**

Here are some ideas for an effective closing to your speech:

- Set out the promise that your core message holds.

- Repeat your key points with a vision forward.
  *"Now that we know 1, 2, and 3, we can accomplish our next step . . ."*

- Circle back to your opening story.
  *Starting a story in your opening and concluding it at the end creates a sense of completion, satisfaction, and closure.*

- Offer a quote that encapsulates your main idea.
  *You might choose to open and close with the same quote, bookending your speech and taking advantage of the power of repetition.*

- Quote a client, or someone who has already taken the action in your call to action, testifying to its power.

Your closing is your final opportunity to influence and inspire your audience. Ideally, your words will be repeating themselves in their heads, or in conversation over dinner. Leave your listeners feeling energized and optimistic. Leave them feeling empowered to make changes in their personal lives, in their place of business, or in their community. In the 15 or 20 minutes of your speech, you will have made a difference in the world.

# 4

## Animate Your Speech

In chapter 2, you gathered your treasures: personal stories, anecdotes, quotes, arguments, data, case studies, and jokes. Now, we will incorporate those treasures into your speech, adding flavor, interest, surprise, entertainment, and emotional engagement in your listeners. We will build out the framework you've constructed into what I call a full-spectrum speech—crafted to reach listeners who respond to different types of material and learn in a variety of ways.

As a high school dance educator, I used project-based teaching. Each semester, I would choose a theme, such as "Dances for a Better World." I created lessons and activities that captured an array of perspectives, opinions, and expressive modalities around that theme.

From a fact-finding perspective, we'd spend time in the library researching a topic of the student's concern. From an artistic perspective, students designed a collage that illustrated their vision of a better world. From a lived-experience perspective, speakers from civic organizations spoke to my class about issues facing our community. From these multiple resources, students gained a 360-degree understanding of the problem, as well as possible solutions. The final activity for each student was to choreograph a dance and perform it. Their dances were insightful, multidimensional, engaging, and moving.

As you put your speech together, you will see that some of these building blocks slot into the basic building blocks outlined in chapter 3. For example, one of your key points might take the form of a story, while another might take the form of statistical data.

## Quotes

One of my best friends has a huge memory trove of lines from movies and poignant quotes from great orators, poets, and writers. In my next life, I want that skill. A powerful quote perfectly encapsulates an idea in few words. When you use a well-chosen quote in a speech, you instantly transport your listeners to the nucleus of your core message.

A quote supports your idea through the voice of someone else—and someone well known and admired. If I quote Oprah Winfrey on a topic I believe in, I bring her in like a cheerleader saying, "Yes! I believe this too! We're on the same team!" Top-class cheerleaders bolster your credibility and authority.

A quote also adds a verbal switch. We've heard the cadence and language of your voice. Now we hear someone else's voice, which adds interest and contrast to your speech.

Stretch your idea of where quotes can come from:

- Multiple voices: gender, race, age, status

- Family, friends, teachers, or children

- You! You have your own wisdom to quote!

- Unexpected resources: Dr. Seuss, a song lyric, a movie line

- Something you overheard at the bank, grocery store, gym, or hair salon

Like an essential oil, which also concentrates the essence of something, you don't want to use too much. One quote is very powerful. Speakers who load up their speeches with quotes quickly become tedious.

Make sure any quote you choose relates directly to your core message.

### Story

Stories are a leading force in marketing, commercials, community meetings, and speaking events. From the TED stage to Creative Mornings, Pecha Kucha, The Moth, and my own company, Story Choreography Projects, speakers are telling stories.

Stories not only live in your heart, they stimulate your brain—literally. As well as activating the language parts of the brain, hearing a story also activates the sensory regions. Say "apple pie," and the olfactory cortex starts buzzing. Say, "stubbed my toe," and we feel a vague sensation of pain even though the nerves from the toe aren't firing. Thus, your listeners are physically experiencing the story as you tell it.

Added to that immediate sensory experience are the experiences from their own lives that your story calls up in your listeners' minds. That's important, since a central goal of your speech is to build an associative bridge from you and your message to your listeners. When you use story well, you create that connection. Add a skillful use of tone of voice, gesture, and facial expression, and you'll have your audience fully engaged.

> *"The shortest distance between two people is telling a story."*
> —Patti Digh, speaker and educator,
> author of *Life Is a Verb*

By capturing and exciting our imaginations, stories can convey a message that, stated baldly, might feel didactic or sentimental or trite. A well-told story might even reach a listener who is philosophically or temperamentally opposed to what your core message is proposing. But it's important to realize that telling a story isn't the magic bullet that makes a speech effective. It's just one rich and potent ingredient.

Here are some guidelines for using stories in your speech:

**1. Make sure your story serves your core message**
You have a message to express, information to relay, a call to action which you want to inspire your listeners to heed. Any story you choose to tell is, first and foremost, a tool to reinforce your core message.

This is not story time. Your goal is not to tell the story as well as it can be told—but to tell it in the way that most powerfully serves its purpose in your speech. So cut away any elements of the story that may be wonderful in themselves but don't relate to your message.

**2. Paint a picture for your audience**

- Land your story in time and place.
  *"It's 2011. I'm sitting in my studio apartment in San Francisco."*

- Give us the details.
  *Color, size, weight, smell, sound. Choose a few key details, just enough to bring the moment to life.*

- Stimulate our multisensory brain cortexes by using adjectives.
  *Yellow raincoat, steaming coffee, itchy sweater, tightly crossed arms, distant stare.*

## 3. Speed up your story

You've heard the saying, "To make a long story short . . ." Keep it that way! A story delivered with momentum is fun to listen to. Hone it down to the essential elements. Leave out all but a few vivid details. And don't go off on a tangent.

## 4. Convey the emotional state of the people in the story

Stories are expressions of our shared humanity. They connect us through emotional experience. Rarely is there only one person laughing or dabbing their eyes with a Kleenex. Make your listeners feel what the people in the story you're telling are feeling. Here are two simple examples:

> "She hesitated before stepping into the line—uncertain if this was where she belonged."

> "When I walked into my mother's hospital room, the tension in my body released and my heart lit up. She was wide awake, her face was bright, and she said in the loving tone I knew well, 'I'm so glad to see you.'"

The power of stories is that they change the dynamic from "you and me" to "we."

## Data

I have a confession: I almost failed algebra in high school. But when I took a statistics course in college, I loved it. The professor pulled back the curtain and gave us an insight into how studies are conducted, who funds them, and what results really mean.

When a speaker refers to hard data, such as a scientific study or statistical information, I'm drawn in for two reasons: first, because it indicates that the subject is worthy of academic study, and second, because it suggests that the speaker has a deep knowledge of the subject.

There are many groundbreaking ideas being shared around the world. When you demonstrate that your core message aligns with the work of other experts, you add credibility to your own expertise. There is strength in joining with thought leaders and weaving in their ideas with yours. This is the benefit of collective sharing rather than competition.

**Connect statistics with story**

After I delivered a presentation about the benefits of story to a nonprofit organization, an audience member asked, "But how do I offer story, when my board of directors needs the numbers?" I answered by using the wise words of Bryan Stevenson, executive director of the Equal Justice Center: "You need data, facts, and analysis to challenge people, but you also need narrative to get people comfortable enough to care about the community that you are advocating for. Your audience needs to be willing to go with you on a journey."

As Stevenson says, "This is a one-two punch: open the door with a story and then follow up with the data." The story captures the human element of the data, and offers a real-life proof of the statistic before you even give it. It anchors the data in lived experience, emphasizing its importance. The technique works the other way round, too: cite the data, and then describe how it is experienced in the real world.

When data is connected with story, information that might seem dry and brain-taxing becomes easy to follow, relatable, and entertaining.

**Make statistics relevant**

Let's say you're not using a story to introduce your statistical data. Don't assume that your listeners will understand the import of the data the way you do. Make the data real to them. For example, if you're including a statistic showing that about 50% of people don't get enough sleep, you might say something like, "Look around—that's equivalent to half of this audience who are burning the midnight oil." You've just done your listeners a huge favor, by translating abstract data into something they can see right there in front of them.

Here's another simple example, from my brother, who is a professor of environmental biology at the University of Maine. To help his students understand the size of a *Tyrannosaurus rex*, he tells them that its tooth is "approximately the size of your foot."

And one more: a double whammy. Wanting to express the urgency of his report, a NPR journalist said, "During this two-minute segment, ten football-field-size sections of rainforest will be cut down." He gave his listeners a reference point for both time and space, making it easy for them to understand the speed at which the rainforest was disappearing.

**Case studies**

Your speech may not call for scientific support, or maybe hard data isn't appropriate to the subject matter. Case studies or client experiences do the same work: they ground your message in fact. By sharing a client's problem, the solution you brought to the table, and the outcome that resulted, you illustrate the effectiveness of your core message in the real world.

**Impromptu data**

You might create rough statistical data right there in the room by posing a question and asking for a show of hands. Or you might make use of an app that allows the audience to sign in and take a poll in real time.

But don't overdo it! At one event I attended, the speaker barraged us with requests to raise our hands. Ten minutes in, I felt like my arm was going to fall off. This is an excellent way to irritate and alienate your audience. And what was worse, the speaker opened with it.

## Transitions

I'm from Asheville, North Carolina, the home of Appalachian culture. My bedspread is a quilt I bought in a small mountain town called Hot Springs. The quilters connect multicolored, multi-patterned pieces of material into a single functional yet beautiful spread. Binding each swatch of material to the next is a thin, barely detectable thread.

Transitions serve that function in a speech, joining the various building blocks into a smooth continuity. Easy, authoritative transitions make your audience feel that you are in control of your subject matter and that you are a reliable guide. They give your speech coherence. Most importantly, they focus your audience's attention. A transition such as "Let's take a look at how these issues affect our community" cues the audience that the speech is moving into a new section and puts the facts and figures that follow into context.

Here are some examples of concise, clear transitions:

- "Now that we have established these three strategies, let's look at how we implement them."

- "For now, I'm going to divide the pursuit of self-improvement into two categories . . ."

- "Let's return to the idea of _____ and see how all this fits together."

- "So, what's next?"

- "This leads us to the final step."

- "Let's take a moment to reflect."

- "Before I close, I want to leave you with . . ."

Don't be afraid to speak plainly. While parts of your speech may employ a heightened language, it's good to stay down-to-earth. Clear transitions mean that your listeners don't have to work to keep up with you. They can sit back, confident in your driving, and enjoy the ride.

---

*Tip: Make sure the elements of your speech flow smoothly from one to the next*

---

**Predictive transitions**

A predictive transition anticipates your audience's thoughts and answers their question without them having to ask. By eliminating these unspoken, maybe not entirely conscious concerns, you're indicating that you are one step ahead of your listeners. This underscores your expertise.

Embedded in this strategy is the pronoun "you." Using the word "you" makes a speech feel more personal and conversational. When you predict your listeners' concerns or questions, they feel understood. Here are some generic examples of predictive transitions:

- "You're probably wondering why I suggest these three steps. Here's why."

- "You may be thinking, "Why [this] instead of [that]?" Let me explain."

- "I know you're asking, 'What are the challenges?' We've asked that, too, and here's how we plan to meet them."

**Audience participation**

A 2005 survey conducted by Cause Communication discovered that an audience's desire to interact with the speaker and their fellow listeners is "strong and, unfortunately, usually unfulfilled." You already know how important it is to establish a personal connection with your listeners. Actual interaction between speaker and audience cements this bond. Audience members are a resource, too: they bring ideas, life experience, and insights.

Your audience hasn't come to be talked at or lectured to. They've come to listen to you, of course; but they're not expecting to be passive. They're expecting to be inspired, moved, motivated, and informed. They're hoping to share in your enthusiasm for your subject. They're hoping for an *experience*. You will satisfy that hope by including them actively in your presentation.

Most people learn best by doing. So, if you can get your listeners to do something, you not only stimulate connection, you provide an enhanced arena for learning.

Some examples of audience participation are:

- Ask the audience a question. Have them raise their hands in response.

- Ask the audience a question, then have them turn to the person sitting next to them to answer it.

- Designate sections of the room as a specific category. For example, you might say, "Those who are most productive in the morning, stand here; most productive in the evening, stand there; most productive intermittently, stand over there." (Warning: don't get people up from their seats if you're limited for time!)

**Break down audience participation into clear steps**

The biggest pitfall here is that the audience might not understand exactly what to do. Both focus and time are lost when people ask questions such as, "Are we both supposed to share or just one of us?"

So, be super clear on what you want your audience to do. Here's a step-by-step breakdown of an audience participation involving inquiry and conversation:

*1. Tell them what is about to happen.*

"In just a minute, I'm going to have you stand up and find a partner. When you find your partner, raise your hand. When you hear the bell, please give me your attention."

You've given them three steps: enough to move your process forward, and not too many to remember.

*2. Direct them to begin those three steps.*

*3. Ring the bell like you said you would, then give your next instruction.*

"Raise your hand if you are willing to go first."

This seems very simple, but note how it compresses information into the instruction. By saying "go first," you've made it clear that both partners will share, in turn.

*4. Tell them what to do.*

"Partner 1, you will share with Partner 2 for two minutes about [the subject under discussion]. Partner 2, your job is to listen."

Make sure to give clear instructions to both participants, and set a time limit.

*5. Explain how the transition from one partner to the other will take place, and how the exercise will finish.*

"At two minutes, you'll hear the bell. Partner 1, please stop where you are. Partner 2, now it's your turn to talk. After two more minutes, you'll hear the bell again. Please return your attention to me."

*6. Give them the cue to start.*

"Let's begin."

Whether you consider including audience participation will depend on the purpose of the event and the amount of time you have. It is not a component of most speeches, and it is usually more appropriate in an educational scenario. Be aware that it requires far more time than what you're allotting for the actual activity; people-wrangling eats up the minutes! Audience participation also requires an assertive speaker, so it's not a good choice if you're feeling nervous or have trouble telling people what to do.

---

*Tip: Be very generous in the time you allot for audience participation*

---

## Q & A

You've just heard a fascinating, inspiring speech, and now there's an opportunity to ask the speaker questions. Lots of people raise their hands. You're enjoying the speaker's thoughtful, engaged answers, but you're also excited to move on with the knowledge and mental breakthroughs you gained in the last 20 minutes. There was a strong call to action—and you're inspired to act.

As the speaker answers the seventh question, your excitement starts to wane. Your heart sinks as you notice even more raised hands, and there's no indication that this won't go on late into the night.

As the speaker answers the eleventh question, you feel like you've been taken hostage. Your inspiration bubble has burst. Your enthusiasm has totally drained away. All you want to do is leave and never think about this subject again.

If you've ever suffered through a scenario like this, you don't need me to tell you that you don't want to let it happen when you give *your* speech. But how do you prevent it?

There are two different ways to include a Q & A in your presentation. As long as you're clear on the difference, and which kind is appropriate for your presentation, you can stay in control of the situation at all times.

**Option 1: The Q & A is an integral part of your presentation**
In this scenario, you will break away from your speech to take questions at a predetermined point, and then resume it. That was the plan in the misfire I described above. The problem was that the speaker gave control of the Q & A to the audience.

*Tip: Never allow the audience to take control of a Q & A*

Keep control by setting clear boundaries on the Q & A. You can limit the questions in two ways:

*1. Limit the time*
Tell your audience, "We have X minutes for Q & A."

You'll need to know your total time limit and how much of it remains, and now you'll have to do some quick math. How long will your closing take? Will you want to repeat some or all of your call to action? Time your post-Q & A closing in advance so you know how long you'll need to do it comfortably, without rushing, with full impact. Subtract that from the time remaining, and you have the amount of time available for the Q & A. Since it might run over slightly, knock a few minutes off before you announce how long the Q & A will be.

Letting the audience know how much time is allotted tells them

a) what to expect, and b) that you will not let the questions run on indefinitely.

If possible, make a prior arrangement with someone to give you a cue when the time for Q & A is up. This is a good strategy for two reasons: a) it can be hard to keep track of the time yourself, especially if the questions are interesting; and b) you absolve yourself of blame for not taking another question. If someone else is seen to be in charge of the timing, you have no choice but to end things, but if you are the one calling a halt, you may become the target of cajoling.

## *2. Limit the number of questions*

You can do this in two ways. If you have only a short amount of time available, you might open the Q & A by saying, "We have time for two or three questions." If you'll have time for more than that, look for a moment that seems to be about two questions away from your time limit and say, "We have time for two more questions."

If the situation allows, you might invite those who weren't called on to stay afterward and talk to you one-on-one (or perhaps email you). Otherwise, they're out of luck. You don't have to apologize for this or feel guilty about it; there's simply not enough time for everyone to get individual attention.

When the Q & A is over, step back into your presentation. This is a change of attitude—maybe a change of posture, or position, or vocal pitch. The more conversational, intimate tone of the Q & A gives way to the more polished, authoritative tone of your speech. You may want to summarize any interesting questions and answers, if they have added a new dimension to your presentation—and if you have time! Then, move into the remainder of your speech.

*Where should the Q & A be placed?*
First, and most importantly, avoid ending your presentation on a Q & A. If you've been asked to speak by an organization that structures the Q & A at the end, complete your presentation before the Q & A starts. You have carefully crafted a closing to send your audience away inspired by your core message and your call to action: give it the space to make that impact before turning to the Q & A. You might say "Thank you"—which most speakers say at the end of a speech—and then say, "We have time for a few questions." You could also ask the person who invited you to speak to introduce the Q & A.

Beyond that, there's no hard-and-fast rule on where to place your Q & A. In a business setting, you might introduce a Q & A after your key points to allow for any needed clarification. I usually place my Q & A after my call to action, so that people can ask questions about what further action they can take. Then I conclude with my "vision with wings."

Frequently a Q & A energizes your listeners further to heed your call to action, but just in case it goes off on a tangent, you might consider finding a way to reiterate your call to action in your closing. Here are some strategies for transitioning from a Q & A into your closing:

- "As we move toward the end of our time together, I want to remind you of three actions you can take."

- "I'd like to leave you with this quote." You can follow that with your vision with wings.

- "It's been a pleasure to spend this time with you. As you go about the rest of your day, I hope you will carry with you the message . . ."—and this becomes your vision with wings.

## Option 2: The Q & A comes after your presentation has formally concluded

Events such as author's book readings and candidate forums naturally lend themselves to this option situation. This "follow-up Q & A" is, in theory, open-ended; you can stay all night as long as people are still asking questions. But make sure you're aware of two things: your own stamina and the venue's requirements. You don't want to exhaust yourself or the venue staff, who may have to stay to clean up after everyone has gone. So it's a good idea to set a time limit, say 15 or 30 minutes. If there are lots of questions or an interesting discussion develops, move it to a nearby café or bar.

---

*Tip: Give the audience permission to leave before beginning a follow-up Q & A*

---

The vital thing in this scenario is to make a clear distinction between presentation and the follow-up Q & A, so that anyone who wants to leave can do so without seeming rude. You might simply say, "Thank you for coming. I'm happy to stay on for 15 minutes if anyone has any questions," or you might give the Q & A a running start by saying something like, "I have some questions submitted in advance that I'll answer first, and then I'll stay on to answer any additional questions." It's a good strategy to prepare a few questions yourself, to have in reserve.

The key to both these Q & A scenarios is to stay in control of the situation at all times; never let the audience drive your Q & A. When you maintain seamless command of your entire presentation, from the opening to the final word, your audience perceives you as confident, authoritative, and someone who is capable of conducting a group of people with clarity and consideration.

A well-conducted Q & A is interactive, engaging, and sometimes delightfully entertaining. It can be an opportunity to let your hair down with your audience, to crack jokes, to get more personal and intimate. In situations such as a conference or workshop, it is a vital part of a presentation. In others, such as an author's book reading, a business pitch, or an introduction to upgrading a business strategy, it's appropriate and welcomed. A Q & A allows your listeners to understand your presentation in greater detail—which could be the deciding factor in whether they buy your product or implement your proposal.

## Slides

Slides are, most often, supporting material to illustrate and punctuate your speech. Occasionally, as in a Pecha Kucha, they provide the speech's structure.

When you use slides well, you create a perfect harmony between what you say and what you show. The audience enjoys a fully rounded experience—like sitting down to an excellent meal at a beautifully set table.

But be aware of the potential for cognitive overload. A speech is a sensory experience on multiple levels: the meaning of the words, the appearance and body language of the speaker, the memories and emotions the speech calls up in the audience. So when you add in visual images, make sure they're not overwhelming your listeners with more than they can comfortably take in.

*Tip: Slides should support your connection with your listeners, not compete for their attention*

The best use of slides is when a picture is worth a thousand words—in other words, when the image makes an immediate, visceral impact. For example, if you are discussing deforestation, you might show an image of the devastation of a clear-cut section of rainforest. Use slides:

- to demonstrate the effect of a key point in the real world
- to convey a statistic in visual form
- to emphasize a key word or phrase, such as "community"
- to emphasize a quote
- to evoke emotion in your audience, such as a photo of someone holding a newborn child or a neighborhood burned to the ground by a forest fire

Don't rely on slides to give important information. For example, it's fine to repeat a statistic on a slide, but don't expect the audience to read the slide while you're saying something else. The bridge you built between yourself and your audience in the opening gives your spoken words more power than anything written on a slide.

*Tip: Use slides as an aid, not a crutch*

Keep your slides simple. A slide that isn't understood in a flash creates overload. You don't want your listeners to expend effort on understanding a slide, because then they're not paying attention to your words. Here are some guidelines:

- one idea per slide

- limit text to a few words, where you want to emphasize a key word or phrase, or a quote

- use clear, high-quality, easy-to-understand images with an obvious focal point

- design text slides with plenty of blank space, so they don't look packed

- keep the graphic design style consistent, in color and font

When you use words on a slide, don't read them out. Let the slide punctuate your words by appearing on the screen behind you, but keep your own attention firmly on your own words and your listeners.

Here are some other mistakes to avoid:

- Don't start your speech with slides. Build the bridge between you and your audience and introduce slides only once you start unpacking your ideas.

- Don't use more than one slide to make the same point.

- Don't write out an entire key point on a slide.

- Don't be overly literal with your slides. I attended one presentation where the speaker said, "And then I parked in the parking lot," and showed us a photo of the parking lot through his windscreen. He also included a slide of the gas station where he filled his tank.

- Don't just stand there describing the image on a slide.

- Don't turn your back on the audience to read out a chunk of text on a slide. (Did I mention, don't *put* a chunk of text on a slide?)

- Don't just stand there in silence while you allow the audience to read your slide. (Did I mention . . .?)

- Don't use slides during your call to action or your closing. You want your listeners' entire focus to be on you at these crucial moments.

**Timing of slides**

I'm often asked, when you do bring up a slide—before introducing a point or idea, or after?

There's no hard-and-fast rule here. As you rehearse your speech for a test audience (or video it for yourself), experiment with what feels best. Usually it's best to introduce the idea or point, then bring up the slide to illustrate it. But it's also possible to introduce an idea by showing an arresting image and then explaining its relevance.

**Using slides to structure a presentation**

Pecha Kucha, a forum for community members to share their passions, is a very demanding, slide-based format. It requires 20 slides, which are up for 20 seconds each, making each person's speech 6 minutes and 40 seconds long. The slides flip over on this rigid schedule. It's up to the speaker to keep up with them.

Because slides are so central to a Pecha Kucha presentation, it's best to structure your speech around them. Choose slides that tell your story—moving the story forward a beat with each successive slide. It's tempting to use multiple slides to illustrate the same point, but if you do that, your speech loses momentum, because every slide is up for 20 seconds: no less, no more.

You can still follow the hourglass shape for your speech, but the rhythm of your speech has to adapt itself to the rhythm of the slides. If it takes you 30 seconds to make a point, your audience's attention will be diverted by the slide changing over. Ideally, you want to be finished making each point just before the next slide pops up—or just before the second-next slide pops up. And you want your timing to be so tight that your speech ends just as the final "Thank you" slide comes on the screen.

The only way to create this synchronicity between words and images is to practice relentlessly and cut ruthlessly. We'll talk more about cutting and polishing your speech in the next chapter.

And don't be tempted by the possibility of just staying silent while the audience enjoys the pretty picture on the slide! It will seem as if you are unprepared or have lost control of your presentation. The audience will no longer perceive you as authoritative and competent. Make sure you have something new and relevant to say as each slide pops up.

# 5

# Polish Your Speech

You've got a draft of your speech. It's not final yet, but it's starting to feel presentable: you've got the right components, and they're in the right order. You've got an attention-grabbing opening and an emotional, specific call to action. You've stuck closely to your core message, and you've focused that message so that it is most beneficial to your audience.

The next step in moving your speech to completion is to polish it. But before you do that, check your timing. You don't want to spend time polishing content you may have to cut because your speech is too long.

## How to Time Your Speech

Read your speech aloud, exactly as you'd deliver it if you were doing it for real. Stand up. Project your voice so that it fills the room. Speak a little more slowly than you normally would. Pause briefly to let your important points sink in. Pause at points where you're expecting laughter.

Don't cheat on this. The only way to get an accurate timing is to deliver your speech for real. If you just sit at your desk and read it through, speaking aloud but without conviction, you'll almost certainly go at a faster pace. And believe me, unless you are unable to stand, you will not have the same conviction sitting down as you have standing up.

Delivering your speech with full commitment will also give you a very valuable authenticity check. You'll feel in your gut if you're not saying exactly what you want to say. Anything that feels inessential, fuzzy, fake, or forced needs to be cut or rewritten.

Time your speech with the stopwatch on your phone. If you've come in under your time limit, congratulations . . . although if you're way under, you might want to consider adding material. If you're too long, you'll have to cut.

Do not even consider solving the problem by speaking more quickly! Cut your speech. You may be surprised to discover that the cuts make it more powerful and dynamic.

**Techniques for Cutting**

1. First, look for places where you're repeating yourself—saying the same thing in different words. Ask yourself, "What's the most powerful, succinct way to say this?"

2. Next, go to any stories. Can you remove some details or plot steps? One of my clients took a four-minute story and distilled it to two—which sharpened the point she was making by telling it.

3. Are you including a "Why Me?" building block? Does it repeat information that your listeners will be given by some other means: the person introducing you, the program, the flyer or email asking

them to attend? Can you request that information currently in your speech be provided to your audience by other means?

4. Look for wordiness. Can you use three words to convey what you're currently conveying with ten?

5. Check for an abundance of "and"s, "because"s, and "but"s. When you remove them, your delivery speed and audience retention will increase. Short sentences are easier to deliver and easier to comprehend.

6. Does your call to action have multiple elements? Can you cut one or more of them?

7. If all that wasn't enough, you may need to remove a story or a key point entirely.

Now that your speech is down to length, it's time to make it as good as it can possibly be. Having read it aloud, you'll have a sense of what sounds natural and what sounds stilted. Written language and spoken language are not the same, and while your speech won't sound as if you're having an everyday conversation, it should sound natural as spoken. Your listeners don't want to hear you reading aloud words that belong on a page.

## Adding Flavor

### Metaphor

At the beginning of chapter 3, I said, "Listening to a speech is like walking through a museum." In saying this, I was using metaphor to make my concept vivid, relatable, and easier to understand.

Metaphor is, technically, an implicit comparison made between one thing and something quite different—for example, "All the world's a stage." For our purposes, we will also include explicit comparisons, which liken one thing to another, such as "Life is like a bowl of cherries" and the museum analogy that I used above.

Metaphor speaks to those audience members who think in a creative, nonlinear way. Those folks relate best to story, quote, and metaphor, while the more logical, analytical thinkers will connect with case studies or statistics. When you include these different modalities, you are getting the benefits of full-spectrum speaking.

Here are some tips for using metaphor:

**Do:**

- thread a strong, simple metaphor through your speech
- refer back to an earlier metaphor and develop it to show how a new point moves your idea forward

**Don't:**

- mix metaphors
- use convoluted metaphors
- introduce a long metaphor without making the relevance clear, making the audience wonder where you're going with this one
- use metaphors in your call to action

Most importantly, make sure the metaphors you use speak to your audience. For example, if I'm speaking to a rural audience, I won't use metaphors of traffic jams or 24-hour diners. If I'm speaking to an urban audience, I won't say, "It's like going bass fishing," or compare something to a star-filled night sky. The purpose of metaphor is to make your idea real for your audience by bringing it into their lived experience.

*Tip: Make sure your metaphors connect to your listeners' lives*

## Humor

Igniting laughter in your audience ignites new possibilities. Because laughter decreases stress hormones and triggers the release of endorphins, our body's feel-good chemicals, a good laugh can transport someone to a whole new way of seeing the world. By giving your audience a belly laugh, you have the power to relax, uplift, unite, and maybe even change the minds of your listeners.

> *"At the height of laughter, the universe is flung into a kaleidoscope of new possibilities."*
> —JEAN HOUSTON, SCHOLAR AND PHILOSOPHER

Humor humanizes you in a flash. Share a funny story or, even better, tell a self-deprecating joke. When you make gentle fun of yourself, you create an instant connection with your listeners. First, because you are treating them like friends, with whom you can let down your guard; second, because it makes you seem humble, not trying to be superior to your audience; and third, because we all make silly mistakes or ridiculous gaffes and have unfortunate memory lapses, your listeners may recognize their own experience in your words.

People are hungry for authentic connection. Humor removes the veneer you might be projecting and makes you accessible to your audience.

Poet Maya Angelou said, "I've learned that people will forget what you said, people will forget what you did, but people will never forget how you made them feel." Make people laugh, smile, or giggle, and you will be remembered with delight.

The most important consideration is to make sure your humor is appropriate for your topic, for the event, and for your audience. Be sensitive to the cultural moment. For example, we are in the age of #MeToo, and numerous cultural shifts are taking place around language.

Here are some more guidelines for using humor effectively in your speech:

- Just like a story, a quote, or data, humor must connect directly with your core message. Otherwise, you'll seem like you're trying to be a stand-up comedian.

- Return to Key Question 2: "Who are my listeners?" Will they get the joke? Does it rely on specialized knowledge or education that they may not have? Ask yourself whether might they find it offensive rather than funny—even if that possibility offends *you*. Don't risk it. The benefit is minor and the downside is devastating.

- Try out your joke or humorous story on friends and colleagues. Choose people who will be honest with you about whether it's actually funny or might be offensive. Choose people from as wide a range of life experience as possible—and be sure to choose people who are representative of your audience.

## How to deal with audience laughter

When the audience laughs, pause. Don't ignore the laughter and talk over it. Doing that is the equivalent of flushing your next statement down the drain.

Accept the laughter as a gift. You've given your listeners a gift by making them laugh. Now they are giving you the gift of hearing their enjoyment of your story or joke.

Start speaking again *just before* the laughter dies away. As the room gets quieter, choose a moment when you'll have to raise your voice only slightly to be heard above it. The sound of your voice as you pick up your speech cues the people still laughing that it's time to move on.

But what if you said something funny and nobody laughs? Awkward, right? This is when your nonverbal communication needs to be clean. Don't look disappointed, embarrassed, or thrown off balance. Don't wait for the laughter that isn't coming. Above all, don't repeat the joke or the punchline and ask for the laughter again. Cut your losses and move calmly, confidently on.

## Repetition

"I have a dream . . ." Martin Luther King, Jr.'s speech at the Lincoln Memorial, the culmination of the 1963 civil rights march on Washington, is probably the most famous example of this technique. Dr. King's repetition of that key phrase seared the point and the language into the minds of everyone who heard it. It added rhythm and momentum. As he ramped up his voice with each repetition, the energy and conviction of the speech built up a fervor of inspiration in his listeners.

Barack Obama rose to prominence in 2004 with an electrifying speech at the Democratic National Convention. He used repetition more as a refrain than as a way to drive home a key phrase:

"We have more work to do. More work to do for the workers I met in Galesburg, Illinois . . . More to do for the father I met . . . More to do for the young woman . . ."

And:

"I believe that we can give our middle class relief . . . I believe we can provide jobs . . . I believe that we have a righteous wind at our backs . . ."

Here is Winston Churchill, speaking on June 4, 1940, as Britain was under attack from Germany in the Second World War:

"We shall go on to the end, we shall fight in France, we shall fight on the seas and oceans, we shall fight with growing confidence and growing strength in the air, we shall defend our Island, whatever the cost may be, we shall fight on the beaches, we shall fight on the landing grounds, we shall fight in the fields and in the streets . . ."

And here is my client Lisa, comparing an Alzheimer's patient to Alice in Wonderland:

"Wonderland Alice woke up from her dream still sitting with her sister, listening to a story. Dementia Alice doesn't wake up from a dream because this *is* her real world:

A world filled with uncertainty and things that make no sense.

A world where hallucinations and delusions are common because your mind sometimes cannot separate fact from fiction . . .

A world where you see things that are not real and believe things that are not true . . .

A world where believing someone is out to harm you or steal from you is real, because when you live with dementia, you live with impaired reasoning, suspiciousness, and paranoia.

A world where you become disoriented to place and time; and believe you are living in a different time of your life . . .

A world where your personality may change and you may become irritable, anxious, or obsessed with an idea, like needing to get some place other than where you are; and a world where it feels like everyone is always screaming at you, and you can't understand anything they are saying . . ."

You might also look back at Kamala's words quoted on p. 62. See how she repeats "We don't want" and "We stand for . . ." and how the repetition of "We stand for" adds impact to her invitation to "Stand with us"—which leads directly into her call to action.

## Assess Your Progress

As you work on your speech, aim to make your language succinct, clear, and emotionally direct. Your message is like an arrow moving directly toward a target: your listener's ear. You may find it helpful to keep these questions in mind:

- Is there a clear line to follow through the speech, or is it disjointed and filled with tangents?

- Does each element follow naturally from the one before?

- Is this statement strong or wishy-washy, with "iffy, possibly, sort of" language?

- Am I using active verbs?

- Am I using inclusive language such as "you," "we," "our," and "let's?"
  *If you find you are using mostly "I" or "my," refocus your speech to address your listeners.*

- Have I used jargon or technical terms this particular audience may not understand?

- Can I say this more powerfully, more directly?

- Is this transition clumsy?

- Does a move from one building block to another feel choppy, as if a transition is missing?

Here are two examples of how to streamline the language of your speech. See if you can figure out what the edits might be before you read the edited versions. If you speak both versions out loud, you'll hear the strength and momentum of the edited, distilled material.

## Example 1

*Unedited version:*

> "In a sense, that's what you're in the process of doing right here and now: transforming a required CME activity into something that is actually relevant and life-giving for you and your clients!"

*Edited version:*

> "That's what you are doing right here, right now: transforming a required CME activity into something relevant and life-giving for you and your clients!"

*What I edited:*

- "In a sense" is vague. Have confidence in what you're saying!

- "In the process of doing" is just wordy. Plus, the sense of transition is covered by "transform" in the very next sentence. Keep your phrases strong and declarative.

- "Actually" is wishy-washy. There's no need to sound apologetic.

## Example 2

*Unedited version:*

> "We believe partnership—with our clients, with our colleagues, and with our communities—is fundamental to

the effective pursuit of transformative design. Our transdisciplinary team of planners, architects, engineers, and interior designers work as partners with our clients to shape ideas that transform our world."

*Edited version:*

"Partnership is fundamental to transformative design. Our team of planners, architects, engineers, and interior designers works with our clients to shape ideas to transform your world."

*What I edited:*

- "We" removed from the opening. Don't start by speaking about yourself.

- There is a strong statement hidden in too many words in the first sentence. Get to the point!

- "Transdisciplinary" removed. Keep your language simple for audiences outside your field.

- Changed "our world" to "your world." Again, use inclusive language to connect to your listeners. Make your speech about them.

As you polish your speech, you'll almost certainly end up with fewer words. If so, great! Seize the opportunity to incorporate pauses. When you make a point, let your words sink in. Don't rush on to the next thing. Give your listeners a moment to comprehend what you've just told them before moving on.

## The value of pauses

In the movie *The Big Short,* Ryan Gosling's character stands at a packed boardroom table, methodically building a Jenga structure nearly two feet high. Then, with a flourish, he knocks it over. One man asks, "What is that?" Gosling pauses. He looks at the man who spoke. He looks at the other men in the room. He looks back to the blocks splayed out across the table. Finally he answers, "That's the housing market." The moment was so powerful they used it in the trailer.

A speaker who is willing to use the dynamic power of the pause garners attention and respect from the audience. A well-timed pause demonstrates control, calm, and command over your presentation.

---

*Tip: Identify places to pause as you rehearse your speech*

---

Don't be afraid to pause with that air of calm command. It does not betray nervousness or a lack of preparation, as novice speakers worry it might. If you try it without sufficient rehearsal, it may feel like an eternity, which you might be tempted to fill in with "um" or "uh"—annoyingly meaningless words that actually do reveal nervousness and lack of preparation.

The benefits to your audience of a well-executed, confident pause are numerous. Pausing:

- adds spice to your vocal rhythm

- adds drama to your presentation

- coaxes your listeners to lean in, meaning that

they energetically move toward you rather
than you having to reach out to them

- gives your audience a moment to catch up with
the meaning of your words and integrate it into
their understanding of your core message

There's also a benefit to you, the speaker. When you pause, you can inhale and, therefore, when you resume speaking you'll have a stronger, more resonant voice.

# 6

# Rehearse Your Speech

You're almost ready to go! Are you feeling nervous?

Probably you are. That's normal. So the final step is to rehearse.

Knowing your content well, feeling the order of your ideas flow naturally, and feeling connected to your words are the tools that will calm your nerves. The way to hone those tools is by rehearsing. Rehearsing will give you confidence, and free you to be all you can be: powerfully professional.

Rehearsal serves two purposes. First, to get you to a place of comfort and confidence. Second, to bring your message to life. Rehearsal is what will ensure that you sparkle. Don't miss the opportunity to make a strong impression, nail your message and delivery, and accomplish your goals!

## Create a Customized Speech Map

Some experts believe that close to 65% of us are visual learners. We respond and learn best when images, graphs, or diagrams are presented. The customized map is a perfect tool to anchor your speech in your memory.

Cheryl, a highly acclaimed speaker, came to me for help before giving a speech at Asheville's speech series Creative Mornings. Her delivery was polished; compelling stories illustrated her main points; humor was sprinkled throughout. All I could offer, at that point, was praise. But Cheryl was concerned about the format of the event. She was used to having a podium, on which she could place notes in case she lost her place. For the first time she would be roaming a stage, and holding notes would look bad. She was afraid she might suddenly forget what came next.

So, we mapped out the architecture of her speech—each building block, in order, and how she had chosen to convey it. Experienced as Cheryl was, she hadn't identified the building blocks of her speech or seen how she'd put them together. She could fly by the seat of her pants in composing the speech, but not in delivering it. She needed a map.

We changed nothing. All we did was map out the speech she'd already created:

- Open with a story
- Move onto information
- Return to the story
- Transition to the history of her subject
- Direct an inquiry to the audience
- Make a call to action
- Close with another story

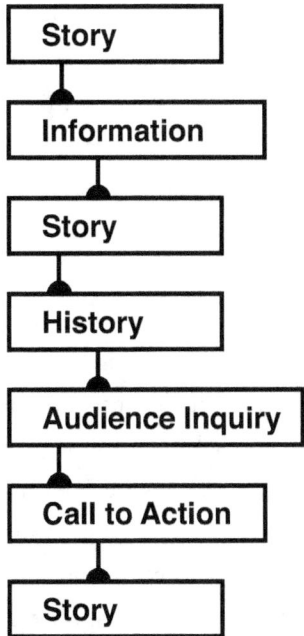

Seeing this customized speech map calmed Cheryl's nerves. She rehearsed with the map in hand, so that its shape became imprinted on her brain.

You may have noticed that Cheryl's map contains a building block that I didn't list above: "history." That's the intelligence of this method: you can identify the components of your speech in whatever way is most useful to you.

Your map will be individual to your speech—and your next speech may have an entirely different map. For example, Samantha starts with a quote. Dylan opens with a riveting statistic delivered in story format. Aubrey offers two key points, while Rick offers three. Melinda weaves a single story in and out of the body of her speech.

*(You'll find more examples of speech structures in the Appendix.)*

I'll discuss below how most people use their map in rehearsing their speech. But here's an idea that you might consider borrowing: Amanda Palmer, a TED speaker, mapped her speech by drawing it on a long piece of paper that she rolled out across the floor. As she rehearsed, she literally walked the building blocks of her speech.

## Memorization

This morning I walked from the living room to the kitchen to tell my husband something, and in less than 10 seconds I forgot what I wanted to say. I had to go back to the living room to retrieve it. Yet two weeks ago, I gave a 25-minute speech without notes.

We all know that memory is fickle. Add in adrenaline, rapid heartbeat, and a grumpy audience member, and your memorized speech may float away to the land of lost socks, never to be retrieved again.

So, you ask, should you memorize your speech?

I encourage you not to memorize your speech word for word. This adds unnecessary pressure, and it usually doesn't turn out well once you hit the stage. You've probably seen a speaker with a look of far-away concentration on their face: that's the look of someone trying to deliver a speech word for word. Consumed as they are with recalling the exact words, they're not connecting emotionally with what they're saying. And that means they're not connecting with the audience.

*Tip: Memorize the shape of your speech, not the words*

Instead, know what you're going to say, and say it however you say it in that moment. Even if it's not precisely as you said it in rehearsal, it will be close—especially if you have rehearsed adequately. By concentrating on the content of your speech rather than the words themselves, you can convey your belief and passion to your listeners.

Adequate rehearsal will set your speech into your bones. You'll know what you want to say as you build block upon block. You will be so familiar with the content that you can conjure it up as easily and fluidly as though you're having a conversation.

## Using notes

If having notes will calm your nerves and give you greater confidence, use them. The most important thing is to inspire and move your listeners. It's counterproductive to lose the connection with them because you're desperately focused on remembering your words and keeping yourself from shaking.

---

*Tip: Refer to your notes, don't read them*

---

I've seen many exceptional speakers use notes, especially in presentations of 30 minutes or more. I've also seen speakers park themselves behind a podium, bury their face in a stack of paper, and read out their speech. There's no quicker way to bore an audience. So if you're going to use notes, make sure you use them as an aid, not a crutch.

Here are some things to consider as you make your decision:

- How long is your speech?

  *Obviously, a short speech is easier to deliver without notes. If it's long (by which I mean anything that doesn't feel short to you), have notes at the ready if possible. Even if you don't use them, knowing they're there will give you comfort and confidence.*

- Does your speech include data, such as statistics, that may be difficult to remember?

  *Have those notes available.*

- Are you using slides?

  *They will serve as reminders, making notes less necessary.*

- How nervous do you get?

  *If speaking is a close-to-fainting experience for you, be compassionate with yourself. Use notes. If you can manage your nerves and feel that you're up for the challenge, step up with courage! Rehearse until you know your speech in your bones, and leave the notes at home.*

- How much notice have you been given?

  *If you were asked this morning to speak at a meeting this afternoon, you have very little time to rehearse. This is almost certainly an occasion for notes.*

Whether you completely memorize your speech or use notes, your delivery should have a flavor of spontaneity. It should feel fresh, authentic, and alive. Your listeners must feel that you're speaking from the heart, not from the page. Your message must be expressed to the audience, not just read from a piece of paper or screen.

*Tip: Spend more time looking at your audience than at your notes*

**Preparing your notes**

Even if you're super nervous, there's no need to put your entire speech in your notes. If there's a story, tell it without notes. (Your notes will just say, "Samantha's story.") If you're talking about yourself—perhaps establishing your credibility—do that without notes. And if you possibly can, make your call to action without looking at your notes. This should be the most passionate moment in your speech—and it will be most powerful if you make it looking directly at the audience.

So, your notes will be memory prompts rather than a full script. By all means put key phrases in them. But you'll get a better result if you are actively generating the sentences that contain those key phrases, rather than reading out whole sentences from the page.

This may sound intimidating. Don't worry. As you rehearse your speech, you'll get used to this technique. I'll discuss how to rehearse in a moment.

Here are some guidelines for preparing your notes:

- Type your notes in font size 14 or larger

- Don't type in paragraphs. Instead, type one sentence per line. (Two or three very occasionally, if they form a single thought block.)

- Use highlighter (sparingly) for important words

- If you're going to be really tied to the page, use a different color of highlighter to mark places where you can pause, look up, and make eye contact with the audience

- Divide topic sections with line spaces

- Headline topic sections, for example: Opening, Key Point #1, Closing

- Number your pages

- Do not staple your pages together

> *Why? Because if you're wearing a microphone, it will pick up the sound of flipping pages. Also, you won't be able to see the top of the next page until you've finished the page you're on, which forces the audience to wait for you to flip over, put your notes back down, and get going again.*

I've helped clients prepare notes and then watched them deliver the speech without glancing down once. You too can achieve this! How? First, by preparing those notes—because that process, too, helps imprint your speech on your brain. And second, by rehearsing your speech, over and over again.

## Polish Your Delivery

You've accomplished a great deal up to this point. Congratulations! You've finalized the content and the progression of your speech, and mapped it so you won't get lost. The deliverables are ready to go.

Now, equal attention has to be given to the deliverer.

You are the ambassador of your business, your project, your art, or your message. You must walk into the room, stand on the stage, or sit at the boardroom table with a state of being that says, "I've got a great presentation. I'm confident. I've got this. You can depend on me." Your words must be as alive as your most committed everyday speech.

In order to create that confidence and aliveness, you'll need to establish a daily rehearsal schedule. How long should that schedule be? If your presentation is due to last 30-45 minutes, I advise rehearsing daily for three weeks or more, in sessions of 20–30 minutes each. A shorter speech requires daily practice as well; one week of concentrated effort will support your ability to deliver it with confidence.

### Establish a pre-performance routine

You will enhance your rehearsal and ultimately your presentation by developing a pre-performance routine. When it comes to doing anything that makes your heart rate increase, your stomach feel like you swallowed a rock, and your brain make an unscheduled departure for the moon, a pre-performance routine is your superpower.

Think of athletes, dancers, actors, radio announcers, musicians. All these people are performing an activity for an audience—just as you are. None of them would dream of stepping on the stage, walking onto the field, approaching a microphone, or placing their fingers on the piano keys without a warm-up.

Nervousness is bound to show up as you approach the stage. It's normal. Many people say, "I'm nervous when I start, but once I get going the nervousness goes away." Even so, before it goes away, if your inner world is not reading "confident, calm, grounded," you don't want to broadcast that to the audience through your nonverbal communication. So, prepare yourself physically and mentally.

Daniel McGinn writes in *Psyched Up: How the Science of Mental Preparation Can Help You Succeed*, "We often feel the most powerless just before we're expected to act powerful." His research shows that people who use a well-conceived and consistent routine perform better than those who don't.

Developing a personally tailored pre-performance routine is a bedrock component of my trainings. This routine will enable you to transform your nervous energy into a focused, passionate energy and an anchored calm. That's the sharp edge you want to be balanced on as a speaker.

I believe that physical preparation is just as important as mental preparation. Your body, voice, and breath are the conduits of your message. So, choose one or two techniques from each category and incorporate them into a routine of three to five steps, in a set order that feels good to you:

**Physical**

- Stretch and shake your body

- Walk, jump, or run

- Take a power pose by stretching your arms above your head and making fists, like you just won a big race

- Open your mouth and eyes big and wide and then squeeze your face tightly closed

**Vocal**

- Yawn

- Breathe deeply and mindfully a set number of times, making the sound "aahhh" on your exhale

- Hum a tune you love

- Overly articulate "unique New York" or "peanut butter and jelly" (I learned the second one from Celine Dion)

**Mental**

- Listen to a playlist of music that is upbeat or calming

- Wear your power tie or sporty shoes—anything that gives you a sense of confidence

- Say a prayer or meditate

- State, with passionate commitment, an intention of how you want to be and how you want to feel

Run through this pre-performance routine before every rehearsal, before networking events, before business meetings, and before delivering your speech.

## Practice your speech

Every time you practice your speech, imagine you're giving it for real. Stand. Project your voice to the far corners of the room you're in. You may want to choose a time when nobody else is home, or borrow a friend's house while they're at work or out for the evening. Maybe you can even find an event space that you'd be able to use when it's empty.

If you'll have a podium, now is a good time to decide whether or not to stand behind it. Your decision will be informed to some extent by the formality of the event, but I recommend not standing behind it if possible, because it creates a barrier between you and your audience. Better to stand beside it (using a lapel mike rather than a fixed mike, if a mike is necessary). Visually, the podium anchors you in space, and you can still place notes or a watch or a glass of water on it. But you are freer to move, and the audience, in being able to see your body language, will connect with you more directly.

Even if you will be standing behind a podium when you deliver your speech for real, feel free to move around as you begin rehearsing it. Walking and gesturing will connect you physically to your speech—which will help you internalize both the shape of the speech and the meaning carried by the words.

As the event comes closer, start reining your movements in. Too much movement is distracting to an audience. They want to see that you're comfortable, not pacing like a caged tiger or gesturing like a ham actor.

When I begin my rehearsals, I print out the speech as I've written it. If I'm going to use notes, I'll create them later. I break the speech into chunks of about three minutes each, and practice them individually. Instead of reading the speech from the page, I glance down for the words and then deliver them naturally. I call this my "refer not read" method. The more I rehearse, the less I need to refer to the page. Once I'm comfortable with the first three minutes, I move on to the next three, and so on. I continue this process until the entire speech feels familiar. This can take a couple of days.

Imagine the words coming off the page, moving through you and animating your voice and body. Connect with their meaning. Feel the emotions. Picture the images. As you become more and more familiar with the flow of your content, you'll feel the speech settling into your brain. Then, each time you bring it out, your delivery will start to feel fresh—almost like you're saying these words for the very first time.

Soon, you'll begin to sense when you need to make a deliberate choice. Choices like:

- This is a great place to pause.

- This transition is an opportunity to make my voice more bold and dynamic, to add emphasis to my next section.

- This phrase needs to be repeated. Saying it once is not enough!

It's not a rational thing, like counting X number of words and inserting a pause. Choices like these should arise naturally from the flow of your speech. You'll hear it, feel it, and understand it's the right thing to do.

After three to five days of rehearsal, put away your printed-out script and replace it with your customized speech map. This way, you can get used to delivering your speech from the prompts that the map gives you, while the image of the map etches itself into your brain. You will reach a point where you'll feel confident that you can call it up in your mind at any moment to keep yourself on track.

Recite the elements of your customized map to yourself while you're washing dishes or doing errands. Knowing exactly where you are in your speech, and what's coming next, will vastly increase your feelings of authority and security.

**Practice with your slides**

As I discussed above, if you're giving a presentation where your slides move on at their own schedule, you will have to rehearse relentlessly to stay in lockstep. If you're clicking the slides forward yourself, you have two options:

1. Introduce a point and then bring up the slide that supports it.
   The advantage here is that you don't want your audience to get ahead of you. Let them hear it from you first. For example, you might say, "Let's move on to talk about modern dance" and then bring up the slide.
2. Bring up the slide and then introduce the point it illustrates.
   This works best when your point *is* the image. You might bring up the slide and then ask the audience, "How many of you remember this image?"

Plan this in rehearsal, and practice until your finger-click is integrated with your words.

Once again, **do not** turn to look at your slides as you speak! Snatch a glance out of the side of your eye if you have to, but you should have rehearsed enough to know where you are if you're clicking the slides forward. If you're doing a Pecha Kucha, you will probably want to check whether your lockstep practice has made you perfect. Some venues provide a monitor—ask about this in advance. Some people place a little mirror on the podium so they can see the screen behind them.

Tech glitches happen—so always be prepared to give your speech without slides.

**Time yourself as your rehearsals progress**

If you're running long, you'll need to edit your content. If you're bang on time, congratulations! But remember, the speech will probably take longer when you're giving it for real. So, you might still want to look for places to cut or reword.

If there's absolutely no possible way to cut, your last resort is to speed up your pace—but I don't advise it. This can be a dangerous business for a couple of reasons: first, because you don't want to seem like you're rushing; second, because you are likely to leave the audience behind and lose your connection with them; and third, because you may not be able to keep to it anyway and may default to your usual pace, thus putting you over time. So if speeding up—perhaps only in certain parts of your speech—is your best option, make sure you rehearse until you're absolutely 100% comfortable with the faster pace.

### Rehearsal techniques

**1. Record yourself. Listen back.**

- Does your voice sound easy and conversational?

- How's your pace—do you sound rushed or sluggish?

- Are you including deliberate pauses, to allow your words to sink in before moving on to the next point or story?

- Is there emotion in your voice?

- Does your voice sound authentic, like you really mean what you're saying?

If your voice sounds dull and expressionless, know you are not alone. I often find that a client will use a calm, expressive, generous voice as we're talking, but as soon as they stand up and begin their speech, their true voice goes out the window, to be replaced by an "I'm-giving-a-speech voice"—forced, artificial, dry, and unemotional. One of my primary tasks with most clients is to help them find their authentic voice as speakers.

*How to bring life to your voice*

First, let's expand the range of your expressiveness. Practice your speech using different emotions. Do your first three minutes in an overly exuberant tour guide voice, the next three in a fire-in-the-belly preacher's voice, the next three as if you're talking to the person you love most in the world. You can make up more voices—as many as you like. Have fun with it!

Please understand that I'm not suggesting you actually speak like this on stage. The point of this exercise is to stretch your voice into ranges that it hasn't yet explored in giving this speech. Doing this will knock you out of the "I'm-giving-a-speech voice" and free you to connect your voice to your emotions.

**2. Practice with an audience**

There's only so much feedback you can give yourself. You know your topic intimately, so the only way to know whether your speech is doing what you want it to do—inform, inspire, provoke curiosity, motivate action—is to beta-test it on someone who has never heard it before.

Invite a friend or colleague, even a small group, to help you. The best people to ask are people for whom you can return the favor—if not now, then at some point in the future. Don't ask people who have a harsh style of critiquing. You don't need this. And don't ask people who will just tell you you're great, either because they're afraid of hurting your feelings or because they love you too much to be objective. Choose people who will give you honest feedback, and give it kindly.

It's okay to give instructions for what kind of feedback you want—in fact, your beta-testers with appreciate the guidance. Make sure you ask for positive feedback as well as negative. Many people don't realize the importance of this! You want to know what's strong about your speech and your delivery of it, as well as what could be improved. This will also bolster your confidence—and that's important.

*Ask for praise:*

- Do I seem comfortable and authoritative?
- Does my voice sound easy and conversational?
- Do you feel emotion at any point? If so, where?

*Ask for performance critique:*

- Am I pacing?
- Am I gesturing too much?
- Do I seem stiff, nervous, otherwise uncomfortable?
- Does my voice sound monotonous or falsely bright?
- Do I seem like I'm hamming it up, or do I seem disconnected from my material?
- Am I rushing, or going too slowly?

*Ask for understanding:*

- Can you tell me the core message of my speech?
- Did I convey it clearly?

- Did the argument or story of my speech follow a natural progression?
- Did you have enough time to take in one point before I moved on to the next one?
- Was there any point at which your attention wandered?
- Was there any point at which you struggled to understand?

The answers to this set of questions will alert you to parts of your speech you want to refine or even rewrite.

*And finally, ask your beta-testers:*

- How did you feel when I finished?

Look back at your answer to Key Question 3: "What do I want my listeners to do, feel, or believe?" Have you accomplished your goal?

**3. Video yourself**

If you really can't find anyone to be your test audience, consider videoing yourself. You can't change what you can't see, and a video provides tremendous insight into what your audience will see.

The first time you watch your video, mute the sound and focus solely on your body language, facial expressions, and gestures. Take notes. Watch again, this time with audio. Keep in mind that it's extremely hard to be your own critic, and most people hate watching themselves—so use this viewing process as an opportunity to make improvements, not to admonish or judge.

# 7

# Deliver Your Speech

Your speech is prepared. Your slide deck is designed. You've rehearsed and beta-tested your speech privately. Did I mention, you've rehearsed?

Before the day arrives, mentally walk through every detail of your speaking engagement, from what to wear to the space you will be speaking in. The more you know what to expect (and are prepared for the unexpected), the more calm and confident you will feel.

## Preliminary Checklists

You can download these checklists at twice5miles.com/downloads.

### Questions to ask before you arrive

1. Who will introduce me?

2. Is there a podium or lectern? If so, am I required to use it?

3. Will I have a microphone? What kind? Ask for a lapel mike if possible.

4. Can we schedule a sound check?

5. Am I presenting from a stage or level with the audience?

6. If on stage, will stage lights be on?

7. Where is the screen located to project my slides?

8. Do I need any adapters to be able to plug in my computer?

9. Should I send my slide deck ahead of time?

10. Can I sell my book or product at the venue, or collect contact information from my audience?

**What you can request**
Depending on the contractual or verbal agreement you've made with the event organizer, you might ask for:

1. A table for book/product sales or newsletter sign-up

2. Water placed on the podium

3. Room set-up with chairs and/or tables in the format most conducive to your presentation

4. Audiovisual equipment

5. An email to be sent to attendees after your speech, with your handouts and resources

Dealing with the details beforehand clears your mind. With no surprises to trip you up, you are free to let go, enjoy yourself as far as possible, and inspire your audience!

## On-site checklist

1. Definitely, absolutely, do a sound check!

2. If there is a microphone stand, familiarize yourself with how to adjust the height.

3. Know how to turn the microphone on—in case it isn't on when you start speaking.

4. Practice your entrance, from your seat to the place where you'll be presenting. Familiarize yourself with any steps, loose carpet, cords, or other pitfalls.

5. If someone is introducing you, consider rehearsing that exchange.

6. Which way will they exit once they introduce you? Make sure there won't be a traffic snafu.

7. Are there parts of the stage which are dimly lit, or not lit at all? Make sure you don't roam into those areas.

8. Is there a clock which you can read easily to check your time? Is it actually working and set to the correct time? (Often clocks in venues aren't maintained, and you don't want to discover the hard way that you've been relying on incorrect information.)

## Things to bring

1. Extra batteries if you're bringing your own microphone
2. Whatever you need for your slide deck: computer, flash drive, remote
3. Cords, adapters, plugs
4. Water
5. A small clock or watch if you have a podium and want to be able to check your time. Put it where your audience can't see. If it's a watch, remove it from your wrist.
6. Anything you need for your promotional table
7. Card reader and extra cash in small bills to make change if you're selling merchandise
8. Breath mints
9. Mailing list sign-up sheet. Create a tidy, professional-looking one; don't just use a piece of paper. Put it on a clipboard. Bring plenty of pens.

## Prepare Your Introduction

One of my first speaking engagements was for a women's organization. The leader took her place at the front of the room and proceeded to read my entire biography from my website. I virtually had to wake the audience up when she was finished.

Fortunately, I learned my lesson early. If someone is introducing you, do everyone a favor and provide them with a *short* introduction. Super short. Highlight only what gives you credibility for this speech (education, experience, volunteering), and one fun personal point.

## What to Wear

Picture this: Three prominent economists sit in a semicircle on stage in front of 1,000 attendees. The woman sitting on the far left has her hair hanging loosely over the right side of her face. More than half the audience cannot see her face.

Picture this: A young, vibrant woman serves as the emcee of a local event. She opens with an uplifting energy in voice and appearance. Unfortunately, three-inch stilettos and a pencil skirt are keeping her legs locked together as she walks on and off stage to introduce the various speakers. She looks like she's trapped in a straitjacket.

Picture this: At a speaking event, I wear a bulky scarf around my neck. (Yes, I did this.) The speech is personal and emotional, but all that bulk around my neck makes me look muffled and closed off. A bare neck and open-necked top would have been a better choice.

Are these make-or-break blunders? No. Are these opportunities to make a deliberate choice that supports your ability to communicate most expressively with your listeners? Yes. Do these elements make an impression? You bet!

What you wear matters. When you speak to an audience, you offer them an experience that is not just auditory. This isn't a podcast. They are seeing you—and what you wear and how you move in your clothing speaks volumes about who you are. You don't want a subconscious message to undermine the impact of your speech.

Here are two questions to consider:

**1. Who's my audience?**
You've already asked yourself this question, when you were preparing your speech. Ask it again as you choose your wardrobe. If you show up in a three-piece suit for an organic growers' convention, at least one person will think you are lost. Arrive at a Women in Business meeting wearing cowgirl boots and psychedelic leggings under a hippie skirt, and your credibility may falter.

I'm not suggesting you wear something that isn't naturally your style. It's up to you to strike the balance between looking and feeling like your authentic self, and aligning your style of personal presentation with the expectations of your audience.

**2. If I wear that, will I feel comfortable and like myself?**
Not too tight, not too loose: find the Goldilocks outfit. Something that's comfortable, lets you move freely, isn't going to slip off your shoulder or compete for your attention (or the audience's). Most important of all: don't wear uncomfortable shoes, no matter how great they look.

### Extra tips

Women:

- Don't wear bracelets or dangly earrings. The movement is distracting.

- If you will be under stage lights, avoid wearing anything that reflects, such as silver or gold jewelry.

- Check under a harsh light whether your underclothes are showing through or creating a visible panty line.

- If you'll be sitting on stage, don't choose a skirt that rises above your knees when you sit.

- Check for tags hanging out, uneven shirt collars, a zipper that isn't fully zipped, or a bra strap peeking out.

- If you will be under lights, add extra makeup, especially lipstick.

**Men:**

- If you perspire a lot when you're speaking, choose a dark-colored shirt and wear a moisture-absorbing undershirt.

- Wearing a jacket? Decide ahead of time: buttoned or unbuttoned. Then leave it alone.

- Check your zipper. Great. Check it twice!

## Speak Like a Pro

You've done a sound check, familiarized yourself with the tech situation, and placed your water and materials where you need them. There are no more details to attend to. Your central focus turns to you—your moment on stage. Now you need to center yourself, and be ready to make the most of this opportunity that awaits you.

Find a quiet corner (maybe the bathroom, if there's no backstage), to do your pre-performance routine. As you prepare to go on, take some slow, deep breaths. Let the air fill your belly and chest. Slowly exhale, and send a message to your body to release any tightness. Feel your feet anchored on the floor, and grow upward from the top of your head. Experience the vertical extension of your whole body as your spine lifts and straightens. Feel big. Take up physical real estate.

Remember why you're here. During the rehearsal process I asked my client Richard, "What motivates you to put so much time and energy into this presentation?" He replied, "I fully believe in my company's ability to provide the best solution and customer service experience for clients. I want these potential clients to know that." That statement captures two elements: pride and service.

You, too, can be proud of whatever you're presenting. Your speech is the conduit of the expertise you've spent years gaining, or the statement of something you're passionate about, or the introduction of an idea or product you've put a great deal of time into developing. Tap into what matters most to you. Feel gratitude for the opportunity to deliver a message that can inspire and transform others. Feel the power of connection.

It's time. With your spine lengthened, walk proudly to where you are speaking. Engage your listeners with a smile and bright eyes. Take at least three seconds to see your audience before you start speaking.

I teach my clients a phrase to say silently during those three seconds: "I see you and I'm willing to be seen." It may feel frightening to know you're being seen; that makes many people feel vulnerable. Accept it. This is your moment to speak, to inspire, to convince, to mobilize. The power of ideas transformed through your voice, your presence, and your purpose can reshape your business, an organization, or just one audience member ready and willing to hear your message, invest in it, and take action to change their world and maybe the world itself.

# 8

# Speaking on a Virtual Platform

March 2020: in a flash we went from shared space to square screens, as meetings, presentations, and rites of passage landed in virtual platforms like Zoom, Teams, and Google Meet. In the course of a year, we scrambled, adapted, and clarified best practices for speaking on a virtual platform.

The experience of a shared virtual space is different in significant ways from sharing a space in person. If you're leading a meeting or workshop, or presenting a speech, it's imperative that you keep certain factors in mind. The virtual space requires greater projection, increased energy, skillful camera use, and a visual frame that indicates professionalism.

As a skilled communicator, your first priority is to build a bridge from you to your listeners. It's essential that they receive and understand your message, feel an alignment and connection with you and your message, and are inspired by the exchange.

## Let Us See You

As a choreographer, I designed dances for the proscenium stage. Lighting, sound, staging, costumes, and placement were always factors in how to form the dance. In the virtual world, you too are in a proscenium frame. So, all the elements of a stage space need to be considered.

**Background**

Virtual communication humanizes you by giving your audience a peephole into how you live. When you speak online, you're welcoming attendees into your home. Make sure it's giving the impression you want to give. What is behind you is, in effect, your stage set, and it can be either complementary or distracting. By decluttering and organizing what is behind you, you will keep your listeners' focus where it should be: on you.

When you choose your location, pay attention to windows. A window behind you throws your face into shadow and may stress your audience's eyes. A window to the side may create a distracting glare or throw an unflattering light on your face. If the timing of your event spans the transition from daylight to dark, that lighting change may create problems.

It's tempting to just place yourself in front of a blank wall, but that can make you look trapped. A bit of depth behind you, with shelves or a side table, counteracts that tendency. One client stands in front of an antique wooden armoire, which gives a lovely warm texture to her background. My friend Amy, a highly skilled facilitator, has one of the most pleasing backgrounds I've seen: books organized by color, a couple of lush green plants, and a decorative vase.

## Lighting

Front light is your best friend. A key light, in front and a little higher than your face, is the most flattering. Ring and cube lights create an attractive glow on your face. If you're speaking during the hours of darkness, ensure that any visible part of the room is well-lit as well.

Start a meeting in your online platform just for yourself and play around with lighting. Place lamps on towers of books or game boxes to find the most flattering angles. (Maybe even put a chair on your desk, and a lamp on the chair seat.) Try positioning a pair of key lights at 11 o'clock and 1 o'clock. It doesn't matter how strange the room looks: nobody will see anything but the proscenium frame you've arranged.

## Camera position

Place your computer so that the camera lens is on a level about two inches higher than eye level. (Again, you'll probably have to build a tower of books or game boxes.) This will ensure that your eyes look open, even when you're looking below the camera at the screen.

Once you've placed your computer, adjust the angle of the screen so your audience can see your entire head, neck, and chest. This looks the most natural. Also, you'll be able to use gestures—and the more nonverbal communication available to you and your listeners, the better.

---

*Tip: Clean the camera lens so that it's smudge-free*

---

When you speak, look into the camera lens. When others are speaking, drop your gaze to watch them speak.

This seems obvious, but looking into the camera can be surprisingly hard. Your instinct will be to speak to the faces you see on the screen in front of you. If your computer is positioned so that the camera is level with your eyes, you'll seem to be looking down or to the side as you look at the people on the screen and you'll have to employ a steely determination to keep your eyes focused on the camera. Simply raising the computer to what may at first seem an exaggerated height solves this problem. Having said that, make sure you make and break eye contact in a natural way. Eye contact is important, but constant, unwavering eye contact is creepy. It's fine to look up if you're thinking or to the side if you're contemplating an idea.

Here are three reasons why it's so important to seem to be looking into the camera:

**1. Eye contact matters—even more in the virtual space**

Eye contact stimulates the social brain—the areas of our brain that respond to others. Though it is nonverbal communication, eye contact speaks loud and clear, saying, " I see you and I'm paying attention." Eye contact promote greater connection. It builds a stronger relationship with your client, colleagues, or audience.

**2. You are in the room, fully present**

At the first session of my "Elevate Your Virtual Impact" training, six-foot-tall Andy had his camera far below eye level. You can imagine how he towered above the rest of us! As I discussed camera placement, he began adjusting his computer. The moment his camera became level with his eyes, we felt him enter the room and become an equal participant.

**3. Your neck will thank you**

Have you heard the term "text neck"? Given the hours we spend looking downward, at a computer or a phone, it's a fitting description. The tightness or pain you feel is your neck and back yelling, "Hey, could you sit up straight today?"

Your head weighs approximately 10 pounds. Drop it slightly forward and your neck muscles are doing all the work. By lifting your camera, you're making a wise ergonomic decision. You'll sit taller, appear more confident, and feel much better at the end of the day.

## What to wear

We don't need to discuss shoes, or for that matter pants—but I sure hope you're wearing more than your underwear. You never know when you might have to stand up!

In order to make the full visual effect easy to receive, keep your clothing simple. Go for solid colors or a simple pattern without too much contrast. Lighten the jewelry, especially anything that dangles or makes noise when you move.

## Let Us Hear You

In the virtual world, nonverbal communication is drastically reduced. This creates a disadvantage for everyone present. In normal settings, nonverbal communication—facial expression, body language—provides under-the-radar information about how your listeners are feeling in the moment. We all use these tools, whether we are aware of them or not. When we don't have them, it's up to the presenter to create as pleasant a communication experience as possible.

The sound of your voice is a key component in the transfer of meaning, influence, and inspiration through a square screen.

**Tech**

Most computer microphones are of high enough quality for virtual presentations—but don't just assume that yours will do fine. If the room you're in is small, your chances are good. But if you're in a large space with high ceilings, you may sound like you're inside an empty water tower or your voice may come through so faintly that you're basically inaudible.

So, well in advance, get online with a friend and get feedback on how you sound. Getting closer to or further away from your computer may not be an option, since it will mess with the visuals. You may need to invest in a lapel mike that connects to your computer through a cable or wirelessly. This is why I said "well in advance"—give yourself enough time to purchase one.

If you're planning to record your presentation for future audio, pay attention to the sound quality of the room. Very possibly there's some echo or harshness. Soften hard surfaces wherever you can, by nailing or taping up blankets on the ceiling and walls, grabbing the cushions from your couch and piling them about, and so on. Just make sure your sound baffles aren't visible in your proscenium frame!

**Tone**

Absorbing and retaining information shared online is more challenging than in person. So, slow your pace of speaking, and add pauses throughout your presentation. Articulate your words clearly. And add a strong, emphatic punch to key words.

## Additional Tips

- Set up a standing desk when presenting online.
  *You will project greater energy and dynamism when you are on your feet. You don't need to buy a new piece of furniture; you can just put a chair on your desk and put your computer on the chair—or build that stack of books or game boxes.*

- Go through your pre-performance routine before logging in.
  *In other words, treat a virtual event in the same way you'd treat an in-person event. Don't feed the cat ten seconds before going live.*

- Notify household members that you have an important meeting and put a "Do Not Disturb" sign on your door.

- Put your phone on airplane mode.

- Turn off computer notifications for incoming messages and emails.

- Move away from your desk between sessions.
  *Get the blood flowing by taking a short walk, outdoors if possible.*

# 9
# Honoring Someone You Love

A toast for a wedding, bar mitzvah, graduation, or any other rite of passage is a huge opportunity to honor those being celebrated and to add meaning and resonance to the occasion. A toast creates connection among families and friends, and brings a tender touch that sends everyone's endorphins into high gear.

Seize this opportunity! It's in your power to turn a lovely occasion into something truly exceptional: a lifetime memory for everyone present.

*Tip: Make your toast as inclusive as possible*

Your toast is a gift to everyone there—not just to the honoree. Make it as inclusive as possible. If your son is getting married, make sure the bride is included in your toast. Talk about the honoree in ways that many people in the room can relate to. Only you have your specific knowledge and experience of this person—but a great toast lets all the guests share in it. So, save the inside jokes for another occasion. Most of all, a great toast conveys your love for the person in such a way that everyone in the room feels love rising in their hearts as well.

## Gather Your Treasures

Just as when you're making any other kind of speech, you'll need to gather some strong material.

Treasure hunting can take many routes. Depending on your relationship and how much time you have to develop your toast, here are some suggestions for starting your hunt:

- What qualities or characteristics do you most admire about the honoree?

- Are there regular actions or pursuits in their life that are significant and meaningful, to themselves or to others?

- Do they follow a tradition that other people enjoy?

- What endearing faults or frailties do they have? Any amusing obsessions or funny habits?

- Is there a phrase they use regularly that you can sprinkle into your toast?

- Which intersections of your life with the honoree's life are the most significant to you?

- Does this rite of passage represent a lifelong desire, or an unexpected turn of events?

- What hopes and dreams does the honoree have for themselves?

- What hopes and dreams do you have for the honoree?

Broaden your perspective: find angles on the honoree that surprise you by talking with their close friends or family members. Ask them why they think this person is special. Ask them what remarkable things this person once did for them.

## Craft Your Toast

Once you've gathered your treasures—stories, insights, outstanding qualities and characteristics, habits and characteristic phrases—you can arrange them into a mini-speech. And when I say "mini," I mean mini! Aim for three to five minutes. Five minutes is the absolute maximum for a toast.

If public speaking terrifies you and this really is going to be a dreadful ordeal, prepare a very short speech, even just one minute long. But still, prepare it! Don't stand up, fumble through a few off-the-cuff words, raise your glass, and sink gratefully back into your chair. Preparing will give you confidence, and you may find it's not as much of an ordeal as you feared.

---

*Tip: Tell stories*

---

Stories are the secret sauce that bring your toast to life. Now that you have amassed a trove of personal qualities, funny habits, or habitual sayings, bring to mind stories of experiences you had with the honoree or know about through your friends that directly illustrate these characteristics.

I recommend limiting yourself to one well-crafted story. With five minutes max for your toast, one story captures the imagination of your listeners and keeps your speech streamlined.

## Choose the right story to tell

Everyone has different lives, different experiences, different relationships, so it's difficult for me to advise you on what to choose. I can only advise on what not to choose: anything that risks being something the honoree doesn't want to have shared in a public setting.

There's a good chance you've known the honoree for years. That's why you've been asked to speak. As with most close relationships, you've witnessed each other's best and worst moments. The two of you may never have overtly said, "Please don't share that with anyone," but it's one of those implicit agreements made from love and respect. So, do not share those worst moments now. However innocuous a certain story may seem to you, you might inadvertently conjure up old hurts, broken promises, or secrets and display them among family and friends. You would be injecting elements of shame, guilt, and embarrassment at the very moment you're trying to affirm, uplift, and celebrate.

These are the four most important things to keep in mind as you craft your story:

**1. Distill your story to its most important elements.**
You can think of this as who, where, when, and what. "What" is the tricky part. To begin with, omit everything your listeners don't actually have to know to get the point of the story. You'll add in a few vivid details later.

**2. Use the phrase "fast forward" to keep the story moving quickly.**
For example: "When Samantha and I were kids, we . . . Fast forward 20 years, and here she is graduating college."

**3. Combine details.**
For example: "Joe and I shared a dorm room, traveled through Europe together, worked in the same office, but today—at this momentous occasion—our paths diverge."

**4. Use words that specifically describe the setting of your story.**
Where exactly were you? What were you doing? What were you seeing or hearing, tasting or smelling, feeling and thinking? Sensory information transports your listener directly into the story—but you don't want to bog down the narrative momentum, so choose just one vivid detail to add here and there to bring your story to life.

## Shape Your Toast

There's no set order for a toast: whatever works for you and for the occasion is great. Still, it's good to have a place to start, so I've mapped out a possible sequence below. Follow this order, or discover your own.

**1. Opening**
People who don't know you want to know your relationship to the honoree. For example:

> "I'm Drew's youngest sister."
>
> "Toby and I were college roommates."
>
> "Alyssa and I met in 1999 at a roller skating rink."

## 2. Include the room

Bring everyone present into the spirit of your toast. For example: "As I look around the room, I see family and friends—a community united in loving Jamie." Or thank the guests for coming and the hosts for creating such a wonderful event. If you are family or close to the family and it feels appropriate, acknowledge relatives who have passed away or who are unable to be present.

## 3. Tell your story

We know who you are. You've acknowledged us. Now is the time to start your story.

## 4. Build a bridge from the story to the future

A toast is a celebration of someone's life so far *and* an expression of hope and good wishes for their ongoing journey. Here you can connect the story, which took place in the past, with the present and the future.

People change—so the person in the story is different in some ways from the person in the present. The changes might be subtle or they might be dramatic. How has the honoree grown, evolved, or changed? What happened to bring them to this momentous occasion?

## 5. Offer a vision for the honoree's future

Keep it simple, and make it bright!

A great way to make your toast inclusive is to say, "On behalf of all of us here tonight, I wish you …" This amps up the enthusiasm, the fellow-feeling, and the emotional power of the toast.

**6. Invite everyone to raise their glasses**
Be sure to include this as you practice your speech. You'd be surprised how many people sit down having totally forgotten the "toast" part of their toast!

## Polish Your Toast

Just as if you were giving a speech at a business or community event, ask yourself the questions on p. 127. And keep one further point in mind: **Address the honoree.**

As you put words together, remember that this toast is addressed to a specific person. Don't talk about them as if they weren't there; talk to them. Use the word "you."

## Prepare to Perform

When a roomful of loved ones raise their glasses in honor of a person, offering a wish or an affirmation of good things to come, it's a powerful moment. The simple choreography of a unison of raised arms, clinking of glasses, and sips of a beverage creates a bond. It's your job to capture this moment: both in your words and in asking everyone to perform this action together.

Be confident as you do this! Imagine yourself as a conductor in front of an orchestra. You are not telling people what to do in a bossy way: you are enabling a collective moment to take place synchronously and smoothly, which is satisfying for everyone. People will be looking to you for direction, so don't disappoint them!

## Practice the toast

When you stand up to deliver your toast, you'll want to leave your notes on the table. Reading a toast interferes with the authenticity and the emotion of the moment. It's okay to glance down at your notes—people will understand if you're nervous—but you want those present, and the honoree, to feel like you're talking directly to them, not reading from a piece of paper.

You'll want to practice for other reasons, too: to check if the content of your toast is strong, to make sure you're within the time, and to feel confident about the moment when you ask people to raise their glasses.

- Find some friends to practice your toast on. If your jokes don't get a giggle, rewrite or delete them.

- If you're running over about 4.5 minutes, trim it. Telescope your story by using "fast forward"; omit some details; possibly omit an entire story if you have more than one. Make sure your vision for the honoree's future is succinct and simple.

- As you practice, decide at which point you're going to pick up your glass. Practice holding the glass, so you'll know how it feels to talk while your arm is raised.

---

*Tip: Hold your glass slightly above shoulder height and not directly in front of your face*

You don't need to memorize each and every word. Know in your bones exactly what you want to say. Practice it enough to be sure of the order of your elements. It doesn't matter if you use slightly different words at the event.

As you practice, especially in the beginning, you may find that you sound dry or "performancy." It's challenging to discover the emotional tone as you practice your toast. Bring up your love for the person as you rehearse; that will make it feel more authentic. At the actual event, your emotions will give authenticity and passion to your words, without effort—as long as you have practiced and feel confident in what you want to say.

If you are looking on this as an ordeal, practicing your speech thoroughly has an added benefit. The more you connect with your love and admiration for the person you are toasting, and the words you're using to express that, the more you will want to convey your feelings to the people who are gathered to celebrate. Practicing your speech not only makes you more confident of the words; it motivates you to enjoy the moment fully and infuse it with meaning. You may surprise yourself, and your loved one, with the confidence and intensity of your delivery!

## Deliver Your Toast

Here are some pointers to make your toast sparkle:

- Make sure your glass is close at hand, and has plenty of whatever you're drinking in it. Take a breath.

- Stand up confidently. Clink your glass with a spoon to get everyone's attention.

- Getting the attention of a large group in party mode takes persistence. You may need help in breaking through the chatter, so enlist the help of others at your table to clink their glasses too. They'll enjoy this.

- Start with a strong voice, loud enough for everyone to hear easily.

- Talk directly to the honoree(s). You're making this toast for the benefit of everyone present, but it is addressed to someone specific: the honoree. Make eye contact. Say their name.

- Talk to everyone in the room. Make eye contact with the honoree(s) often, but don't forget to raise your eyes to connect with everyone else, too. If you think this will make you too nervous, sweep your eyes around all three walls, just above head level. You don't actually have to make eye contact with any individual people.

- Be animated. Use gestures to describe details. Do voices for any dialogue in your stories, mimicking people's tone or way of speaking. But kindly!

- Speak from the heart: Authenticity is vital. Speak from what is true and real for you, from your genuine love and admiration for the honoree. It's fine if this brings tears to your eyes. Take a breath, collect yourself, calm your voice, and keep going. Everyone in the room will feel your emotion, and their own emotions will bubble up to mirror it.

- Smile: This is a happy occasion! Even if you're longing for your speech to be over, don't let people see that. Connect with your emotions, and the smile will come naturally.

- Raise your glass: As you invite everyone present to raise their glasses, demonstrate by raising your own.

- Deliver your wish directly to the honoree: "On behalf of everyone present, I wish you . . ."

A short sip is enough. However much you may feel you need a drink at this point, keep your focus on the honoree—who may well want to hug you.

## What to avoid

When you make a toast, you are in a position of power. You're talking about someone in front of other people, and that person can't do anything but sit quietly and listen. So don't abuse your power!

Here are some examples of abusing this power:

### Got you!

After five years of dating and living together, Rose and Ben are getting married. The mother of the bride stands for the first toast. Everyone is eager to hear her words of encouragement and love for her daughter and her new husband.

Before long, the glow of smiles around the room is dimming. People are squirming in their chairs. The bride is squeezing her husband's hand so tightly that it's turning as white as her dress.

I've been there. You've probably been there too.

***What went wrong?***

- The mother never mentioned Ben. It was a message for her daughter only.

- She thought she was being cute and funny by telling slightly embarrassing stories about Rose as a teenager.

- Her message was closer to "got you" than "congratulations." Her smile was more triumphant than loving.

- She went on way too long.

***Solution:***

- If your toast is for a couple, be sure to include both in your toast.

- A toast isn't a two-way conversation. It's a gift for everyone who listens.

- You are there to uplift the honoree(s), not to make fun of them. However affectionate it may feel to you, this is a public occasion, and nobody likes to feel exposed in public.

## Honoring who?

Cynthia asked me to help her with a toast for her husband's seventieth birthday party. She did an exceptional job of storytelling and highlighting her husband's best qualities. The problem was that the toast was all about how this wonderful, intelligent, generous man had contributed to her life. For four minutes she used the words "my," "mine," "me," and "I." The speech was about her, rather than about him.

*Solution*

• Make sure the honoree is at the center of your speech.

**Salty language not included**

Children might be there. Grandma might be highly religious. Father-in-law Bill may have an aversion to cuss words. To stay in the good graces of all attendees, avoid the salty language.

## Words of Love

I just turned sixty. At a small dinner of friends, my best friend of twenty years stood up and offered a toast. She talked about how we met, how her life had been changed by knowing me, and how she has seen me evolve over those two decades. Her words showed me that she sees the true me, knows my tender spots, and recognizes my greatest gifts. She let me know, without a doubt, she loves me.

We all want to be seen and known. Your toast is just that—a declaration of knowing who this person is, how they touch the world, how they've changed lives, and how much you love them.

# APPENDIX
# Sample Speech Shapes

## The Basic Hourglass

*Scenario:* Your boss asked you to make the case for hiring an additional customer service manager in order to cover an increase in customers. The decision-makers in the company aren't convinced that the expense will be worth it. You've got 5 minutes to convince them.

**Opening**

> You choose a positive opening: statistics that highlight the increase in customers and the company's growth. Your boss and the decision-makers are giving themselves a pat on the back. So, they like what you're saying! They're listening.

**Core message**

> "Because of the increase in customers, I am proposing that we hire one additional customer service manager."

**Why does this matter?**

> "We have become famous for our excellent customer service.

Here's why I believe we need an additional customer service manager in order to keep up the level of excellence our customers respect and expect."

## Key points

1. "Our turnaround time is one day longer than it was before our growth, which means that our customers have to wait longer than they're used to waiting."

2. "Even though our entire staff is working an extra hour every day, we cannot complete the workload."

3. "Employee morale is dropping because of stress and overwork."

## Call to action

In this case, your call to action—hire an additional customer service manager—is contained within your core message. So you can simply remind your listeners of it and then:

## Closing

You set forth a positive and inspiring vision of the company's future if this step is taken—and remind your listeners of that pat on the back they gave themselves earlier. "By approving this new hire, we can meet the demands of our customers with the excellent service that has made us their number one choice. Let's continue to build on our success!"

## Compare and Contrast

*Scenario:* You are presenting a proposal to do away with an old system in your company and introduce a new one.

**Opening**

"When this company meeting was announced, I noticed worried faces. Changes in a workplace can mean disruption and upheaval. Today is different! I believe that by the time I've finished introducing my proposal, your concerns will be transformed into approval and excitement."

**Core message**

"Our physical therapy practice has two guiding principles: to serve our clients and to respect our staff. So, I'm pleased to announce that our practice is poised to reshape our patient interaction and our personal well-being, and streamline the workflow of this office."

**Old system: overview**

"We've been working with an antiquated layout: multiple private rooms, with doors closed, with a computer, desk and PT equipment in each one. This traditional system has many disadvantages:"

**Old system: key points**

- "When you enter a treatment room, you have to

log into the computer and locate your client's file. This is not only an inefficient use of time, it robs time from the client—therapist connection."

- "Our clients are isolated in their rooms as they are moving through their physical therapies. The isolation is unnecessary and is proven to only heal the physical symptoms, not the whole person."

- "We encourage our clients to avoid sitting for long periods of time, and what do we model? We sit there at the computer, documenting our notes! This is not good for you, the therapist, nor is it a good example for our clients."

- "And, because of the layout of these rooms, you have your back turned to them as you do this."

- "Plus, we can only serve four clients at a time."

**New system: overview**

"After visiting multiple clinics across the state, we've become convinced that reshaping the layout of our office will produce better healing outcomes for our patients and create a more efficient, pleasant, and healthy working environment for our therapists. This is what we propose to do:"

**New system: key points**

- "We will create a large common room for PT exercises. Research shows that when clients share a space with others going through their PT, they show greater motivation, commitment, and pleasure in doing their own PT. The inclusive environment is generative and positive."

- "We will maintain private spaces, but they will be divided by curtains rather than doors."

- "Each therapist will be given their own computer standing cart, allowing you to move easily from room to room, and allow you to stand rather than sit."

**New system, benefits, key points:**

"The benefits are many:

- We will have lower expenditures on equipment purchase and repair.

- We will be able to serve three times as many clients as before, which means that:

- We can hire more therapists.

- The increased interaction will foster more of a community spirit, which we believe will uplift everyone's experience of working here and healing here."

## Q & A

"I'm happy to answer any questions about how we're going to make this happen."

**Call to action**

"To begin this transition, we will hold an onboarding

training next week. We'll show you the plans for the new layout, give you training on the new computer system, and walk you through the new processes for client care. Starting on January 23, we'll be moving next door for three weeks while the office is renovated."

**Closing**

"If I'm reading your faces correctly, I believe you are as excited as we are about these changes. Again and again as we traveled around the state, we were told that this kind of working environment created a huge improvement in staff morale. I hope you'll be enjoying your job much more when you are not isolated behind closed doors for much of the day. You'll be moving among your colleagues in a larger space with sunlight and high-level equipment, and you'll be able to interact more personally with your clients and share your gifts of skill, expertise, and client care."

## Chronological

*Scenario:* You are speaking at your college graduation, getting your degree in education. You want to celebrate the power of teachers.

**Opening**

"It takes just one: one teacher who stays after school to help catch you up on the lesson that you didn't understand; one teacher who makes you feel that your ideas are interesting; one teacher who believes in you. Were you lucky enough to have that teacher? I was: Mrs. Bradburn, in sixth grade. Socrates said, 'Learning is the kindling of a flame, not the filling of a vessel.' Mrs. Bradburn not only taught me to love learning—she taught me to love teaching."

**Why me?**

"Attending college wasn't something my family expected of me. My parents got no further than high school. But I was a curious child who loved to explore, discover, and observe. With the help of encouraging, supportive teachers, I was able to win a scholarship to college—and received the prestigious Horizon award for excellence in education in my freshman year. Would that have happened without Mrs. Blackburn? Very possibly not."

**Core Message**

"Teachers have the power to change the trajectory of someone's life—of many people's lives. It's a sacred trust, which deserves to be acknowledged, respected, and honored."

**Past**

"Learning didn't come easily to me. I struggled especially with math and science—and I felt ashamed. The lack of parental support made it even harder. Mrs. Bradburn made me believe that learning was not just possible, but exciting and nourishing. She was the reason I decided that teaching would be my career."

**Present**

"Now, as I complete my final exams and internship, I am poised to influence many young lives through education, guidance, influence, and love. It is a lifelong dream come true."

**Future**

"In three months, I will cross the threshold of Walnut Elementary School and take my place at the head of the fifth-grade classroom."

**What's possible?**

"I hope that I will be able to do for my students what Mrs. Bradburn did for me."

**Call to action**

"I ask you all to take a moment to think again about the teachers who influenced your lives. Do they know how important they were to you? Have you told them of the fires they kindled in you? Imagine their delight in hearing from a student from decades ago, thanking them for the lasting change they made in your life."

**Closing**

"One day, I believe, teachers will take their rightful place among the most honored members of our society. As we remember them, honor them, thank them, we bring this change about. I've invited a special guest here today. Mrs. Bradburn, will you stand up?

Mrs. Bradburn—thank you."

## Speech to honor someone

*Scenario:* You've been asked to speak in honor of someone. This might be a eulogy at a memorial service, or it might be a happier occasion. There may well be no natural call to action: no toast or other group action. But without a call to action, your speech runs the risk of simply tailing off into a thank-you or a statement of how much you loved the person.

Better to bring the person alive with the story you tell. Think of your speech as a little bit of storytelling. Take the audience on a journey into some aspect of the honoree's personality and end with some kind of climax or revelation—like the punchline of a joke. (Humor can be appropriate even at a memorial service. Unlike a funeral, a memorial service is an occasion to celebrate a life rather than to mourn a death.) To make your story more intriguing, look for contradictory qualities in the person you're speaking about, or a way to reverse your audience's expectations.

A friend was asked to speak for four minutes on the occasion of her late father being inducted into the Irish American Hall of Fame. Clearly, her father's love of Ireland would be the topic of the speech. Pacing up and down a Chicago hotel room, she generated the speech by speaking it, focusing on her father's connection with Ireland. He had moved there and taken Irish citizenship in the 1960s, but in fact had considered moving to Italy as well and only chose Ireland because there would be no language barrier. That gave her the pivot on which her speech turned:

> "My father was not born Irish American. Becoming Irish American was one of the greatest achievements of his life."

Of course, he was being inducted into the Irish American Hall of Fame because of other achievements. So asserting that becoming Irish American was more important to him than the fame he achieved in his career was a surprise to the audience, and a much-appreciated celebration of the group's identity.

Now that you've completed *How to Write a Speech*, are you ready to inspire an audience?

You'll find further valuable resources at standanddeliverasheville.com/resources.

And if you'd like personal coaching, join me for my online training, "Craft a Speech Worth Sharing." I will guide you from "throw it together" to "stand and deliver." The result: a speech that captures your most compelling and convincing message through a step-by-step strategic and creative framework.

www.ingramcontent.com/pod-product-compliance
Lightning Source LLC
Chambersburg PA
CBHW051947290426
44110CB00015B/2146